SECRETS FROM THE COCKPIT

SECRETS FROM THE COCKPIT

Pilots behaving badly and
other flying stories

ROBERT SCHAPIRO

JONATHAN BALL PUBLISHERS
Johannesburg • Cape Town • London

Published in South Africa in 2021 by
JONATHAN BALL PUBLISHERS
A division of Media24 (Pty) Ltd
PO Box 33977
Jeppestown
2043

ISBN 978-1-92824-814-9
ebook ISBN 978-1-92824-815-6

*Every effort has been made to trace the copyright holders and to obtain
their permission for the use of copyright material. The publishers apologise for
any errors or omissions and would be grateful to be notified of any corrections
that should be incorporated in future editions of this book.*

www.jonathanball.co.za
www.twitter.com/JonathanBallPub
www.facebook.com/JonathanBallPublishers

Cover by Sean Robertson
Design and typesetting by Martine Barker
Set in Adobe Caslon Pro

Contents

PART THREE: THE JAPAN YEARS

Author's note

Tom Grunnick: 'What do you do when your real life exceeds your dreams?'
Aaron Altman: 'Keep it to yourself.'

— Exchange between a successful TV anchor and an unsuccessful writer in the 1987 movie *Broadcast News*

Good advice, but I'm not going to follow it. I'm going to spill the beans on how the most unlikely person, me, became one of just a few thousand people in the world to end up in the command seat of a Boeing 747 – captain of a jumbo jet.

My career had its costs. I missed many important milestones in my son Morgan's life. I tried to make up for it by bringing back gifts from every trip, but soon feared that was all he was waiting for when I returned home jet-lagged, tired and irritable – my bag with the goodies inside. I didn't get to make some of the important decisions in his life – my wife, Arlene, did that – and I quickly learned it was wrong to come home, interfere and then leave again.

But Morgan always loved my flying stories. He still does, even though he's not a child any more. He'll laugh and say, 'Dad, you've got to write that one down sometime.' Some years after I retired I did just that. To my amazement, I covered page after page of a legal pad – and those were just the chapter headings.

This book is a time capsule of the military and civilian aviation industry between 1975 and 2010, particularly in apartheid South Africa and in Japan. I'm not trying to criticise anyone, I'm just trying to tell readers my flying stories exactly as they happened – or, in cases that were too good to miss, as they were told directly to me by other pilots.

I hope you enjoy reading these stories as much as I enjoyed writing them.

Robert Schapiro

Glossary and abbreviations

Editor's note:

Secrets from the Cockpit follows the widespread international aviation practice of using the imperial system to measure altitude, speed and distance. Fuel is typically ordered in gallons. For readers interested in metric equivalents, a foot is roughly equal to 30 centimetres, a mile is 1.6 kilometres, a knot/nautical mile is 1.8 kilometres, a pound is just shy of half a kilo and a gallon is around four litres.

AGA	Aerodrome Ground Aid (homing beacon)
AGL	above ground level
ATC	air traffic control
ATIS	Automated Terminal Information System
auto-throttle	automatically moves the thrust levers
CRM	Crew Resource Management
DME	distance measuring equipment
downwind	flying outbound, parallel to landing runway
drag	retarding force/friction
engine stall	disruption of airflow through engine
feathering	setting propellor blades into the windstream
flaps	movable surface on rear of main wing to increase lift
flare	raise aircraft nose to soften touchdown
finals (final approach)	last portion of an approach
hold	circle over a fixed point
HF	high frequency, long-range radio

Secrets from the Cockpit

IAS	indicated air speed
idle thrust	minimum thrust, thrust levers closed
ILS	Instrument landing system (provides electronic guidance to touchdown point)
IMC	Instrument Meteorological Conditions
instrument flying	using only flight instruments, no visual references
INS	inertial navigation system
markers	touchdown zone markers
reverse thrust	redirecting engine exhaust gas forward to slow aircraft on runway
sideslip	high-drag yawing manoeuvre to lose height quickly
sink rate	rate of descent, generally feet/minute
speed brake	rising panels on top of main wings
STAR	Standard Terminal Approach Route
RA	resolution advisory
TCAS	Traffic Alert and Collision Avoidance System
TOC	top of climb
TOD	top of descent
VAs	Vital Actions
VHF	Very High Frequency, short-range radio
visual approach	approach using visual references
VOR	VHF omnidirectional radio beacon
wake turbulence	rough air behind an aircraft
windmilling	revolving propeller not powered by engine
wind shear	rapid variations in wind speed and direction

Prologue

It was a regular flight from Amsterdam to Anchorage. Until the fire alarm started blaring.

We'd left the Netherlands on a rainy summer afternoon, planning to fly our Nippon Cargo Airlines jumbo jet via Norway and the North Pole to Alaska. I'd climbed to our initial cruise altitude of 29 000 feet, changed from my uniform into my sweats, made myself tea and was resting my feet on the instrument panel footrests while I watched the Norwegian fjords slowly receding under our right wing. Then came that bell.

The flight engineer turned off the jarring noise. We scanned the engines. All four looked fine. 'Where the hell is that?' asked our captain, a former Trans World Airlines (TWA) pilot best known in the airline for a Mississippi accent so thick even fellow Americans had problems following him.

'Main Deck Cargo,' replied the flight engineer, in a clipped, disbelieving voice.

'Get the checklist,' said the captain.

The checklist, a thick book known as the QRH, or Quick Reference Handbook, provides step-by-step procedures for in-flight malfunctions and emergencies. In this case, there was a simple bottom line: 'Land at nearest suitable airport.'

An onboard fire is one of the most dangerous things that can happen on an aircraft. It's almost impossible to control in the air, so the only response is to get on the ground fast and get the hell out. I already had painful knowledge of what could happen to a burning 747. In 1987, when I was a pilot for South African Airways (SAA), a fire in the cargo hold of an SAA plane called the *Helderberg* caused the aircraft to break up just off the Indian Ocean island of Mauritius. It plummeted into the sea a little more than 20 minutes away from landing, killing all 159 people on board.

Captain Mississippi radioed Norwegian air traffic control (ATC) with just one question: 'Where is the nearest airport capable of landing a Boeing 747?'

'Bergen,' came the startled reply. 'About 180 nm (nautical miles) ESE of your position.' The captain requested immediate clearance to descend from 29 000 feet and to head for Bergen, saying that we had a possible onboard fire. 'Are you declaring an emergency, Nippon?' asked the controller, a procedure that would give us priority over all other traffic. Hell, yes. Yes we were. 'Proceed as requested and descend to 5 000 feet at your own discretion,' he said, giving us a magnetic heading to Bergen and the frequency of the airport's VHF omnidirectional radio (VOR) beacon.

I hadn't waited for the exchange to end before swinging the nose to the right, aided by a healthy push of the right rudder to speed the turn. As soon as I was pointing in roughly the correct direction, I closed the throttle and pulled the speed brake. Down we went with our speed at the safest maximum – known in aviation as being 'on the clackers' because of the system that makes a loud clacking noise if you go too fast.

'Should we dump fuel?' asked the flight engineer. It wasn't really a question: we were at least 100 000 pounds (45 000 kilograms) overweight for landing. 'Yes, do it immediately,' said the captain.

Within moments, two thick streams of fuel were pouring from the fuel jettison nozzles on the wingtips. We were now fully committed to the unscheduled landing.

'Rob, why are you descending so early?' the captain asked as we passed 20 000 feet. 'At this rate, we'll be at 5 000 feet at least 80 miles before Bergen.'

Prologue

With the *Helderberg* in my mind, I'd wanted to be in a position to get our plane on the water quickly if it became necessary. To placate him, I stowed the speed brake and put on a little power to flatten the descent. Then we turned to our next urgent problem. We were heading full speed towards an airport for which we had zero knowledge or information.

ATC transferred us to Bergen approach to get the airport data we needed. We scribbled busily as the Bergen controller gave us airport altitude, runway length and heading, instrument landing system (ILS) frequency, initial approach altitude, missed approach procedure and, finally, current weather.

It was enough to get the jet on the ground – provided we could get to the airport without burning up first.

PART 1

THE AIR FORCE YEARS

Chapter 1
Army Hell

Not a day – sometimes not an hour – of my years in the South African military went by without one of my Afrikaner barrack mates calling me *Jood* (Jew). They weren't saying it to be nice.

One time I took the opportunity for a little payback. They often asked me to speak 'Jewish' (whatever that was), so I decided to tell them what I thought of them in the Hebrew I had learned at my Jewish day school in Cape Town.

At least, I started in Hebrew. But somewhere in my diatribe I drifted into another language. I noticed their mouths dropping open as I was speaking and realised to my horror that I was bad-mouthing them in their native tongue – Afrikaans. I stopped and pretended I'd been having a little joke. No one asked to hear any more Jewish after that.

Like the other young white men of my generation, I had been conscripted into the South African Defence Force for what the National Party government called 'national service'. We were required to serve up to two years – depending on when we'd been called up – and then do occasional stints in the reserves after that. We could choose whether to go immediately after high school or defer until after university, but other options were limited. The small number of my contemporaries who chose to leave the country instead, took the risk of becoming exiles, forbidden from returning to visit their families – a hard choice for a teenager.

I went into the army at 17. My goal had been to go straight into the South African Air Force (SAAF) to train as a pilot –

my dream since the day I started primary school – but when I got my papers, they instead ordered me to report to the School of Engineers at Kroonstad, in the Orange Free State.

I'd always wanted to fly; I cannot remember ever considering doing anything else. One of my father's 8 mm home movies shows me playing vigorously with a model of a silver jet sporting glowing red engines. That aircraft was a Boeing 707, the precursor to the Boeing 747 jumbo jet in which I would later log thousands of hours of flight time.

At school, I talked endlessly about aviation, but few of my classmates or teachers wanted to listen. My brothers and I all attended Herzlia, a secular Jewish day school that emphasised academic achievement and offered an alternative to the 'Christian national education' provided by government schools. Under apartheid, South African schools were strictly segregated, with white schools getting generous funding to provide pupils with decent educations and black schools only getting enough to prepare children for menial jobs. At Herzlia, most of us were the children or grandchildren of those who'd fled the pogroms and persecution of Russia and Eastern Europe, attracted to South Africa by economic opportunity and the promise of religious freedom. Unlike the Afrikaner-run ruling party, we were native English-speakers and tended to be liberal in our political outlook, making us a minority within a minority within a minority.

Still, South Africa was a wonderful place to grow up in. Wonderful if you were white, that is.

I was born in the breathtakingly beautiful city of Cape Town in 1957. Nine years earlier, DF Malan had led the National Party to electoral victory and begun implementing the party's vision of 'separate development' – better known as apartheid.

When you think it's normal to live in whites-only neighbourhoods, ride on segregated buses and swim at whites-only beaches, it takes a while to realise there is something sick and twisted going

4

on in the country. Instead, I believed I was growing up like any other child in places like America, Britain or Australia. Unlike the helicopter parents of today, our parents let us wander round until dark. We explored Table Mountain and the forests and stone quarries close to our house. We felt safe, protected by a police force that rounded up *skollies* and *bergies* (thugs and vagrants) from our protected streets. True, the Afrikaner government didn't allow us to get television until 1976, a year or so after I finished high school, but that only gave us more time to enjoy life outdoors.

I was barely out of toddlerhood when I got my first look inside a cockpit at a Cape Town airshow – and knew what I wanted to be when I grew up.

At Herzlia, my flying ambitions were greeted with scorn. We were expected to pursue professions such as medicine, law or accounting, not to become pilots in the Afrikaner Air Force. I remember one of my classmates sneering as he told me about a high-achieving Afrikaans-speaking neighbour – a head prefect, rugby captain and 'A' student – who had been rejected by the SAAF flight school. 'How do you think they'll ever take you?' he asked.

He had a point. I was less than athletic, somewhat immature, had mediocre grades and, worst of all, was failing in the maths that I needed to excel in to fly. I had a well-deserved reputation as a *loskop*, someone so scatter-brained they'd lose their own head if it weren't attached, and was not good at thinking things through. Once, I designed and built a solar reflector in the basement of our home in order to boil water using the power of sunlight. Only after I had finished it did I realise that the reflector bowl was too large to fit through the basement door. This inability to deal with the details plagued me well into my flying career.

But first I had to start that career. And that meant grappling with high-school maths. My mother hired a series of private tutors to help. One specialised in raiding the fridge while I plodded away at equations in the formal dining room. I kept failing. Then my Standard 7 (Grade 9) class got a new teacher, a neat, fussy man who spoke in soft, staccato sentences and could draw a perfect freehand chalk circle on the blackboard. He somehow made me understand his lessons perfectly. I went from an F to an A in two terms. Ironically, Herzlia never acknowledged my mathematical resurrection – I suspect they thought I was cheating – but years later, I learned that they cited my acceptance as a pilot for South African Airways as an example of what can be done if you persevere.

It was 1975 when I was sent off to Kroonstad. Apartheid laws were firmly in place to keep the races apart. We couldn't attend the same schools or live in the same neighbourhoods, and sex – never mind marriage – between black and white people was illegal. The government was pursuing its insane grand apartheid vision of stripping all blacks of citizenship by ordering them to live in so-called Bantustans, arbitrarily defined ethnic 'home-lands' scattered around the country and ruled over by crony black appointees.

In South Africa's convoluted racial hierarchy, whites were at the top, blacks at the bottom, with those classified as Indians and coloureds in between. Only whites could vote. Only white men were conscripted.

Black people could only legally live or work in South Africa proper if they had special internal documents known as passes or the *dompas*. Police conducted regular roundups to arrest those who couldn't show these papers on demand.

This was also the year that South African soldiers became involved in the civil war in newly independent Angola, where Cuban troops intervened in support of the Soviet-backed communist government in Luanda. South African forces entered the conflict both to influence the political outcome in Angola and to root out insurgents infiltrating South African-administered South West Africa, now Namibia, and to help the US-supported Unita rebels in their ultimately unsuccessful efforts to push the Marxist MPLA out of power. I would have my own role in that conflict soon enough.

I began my military service by reporting for duty at the Cape Town Castle, which was used as a base by the army. The five-pointed shape of the Castle was also the air force's roundel. I lined up outside the historic building with other conscripts, joined the group bound for Kroonstad and walked with them across the road to the city's main railway station. Family and friends waited near the trains to say emotional goodbyes, pressing chocolates and food parcels into our hands. For most of us, it would be our first time away from home.

The 28-hour train ride got ugly fast. The orchard-laden valleys of the Boland quickly turned into flat, dry terrain. When the electric line ended in the semi-arid Karoo, our stuffy carriages were coupled to a steam locomotive and the reward for opening a window became a blast of warm coal dust. Worst of all, thugs among the conscripts ganged up to prey on their gentler companions. Luckily, we pulled into Kroonstad before things got too out of hand – and then the bullies were too busy trying to survive the army to worry about weaker souls.

We arrived at 2 am and were promptly ordered into three-ton Bedford trucks for a bone-jarring ride to the base. This was designed to intimidate us 'roofies' (new recruits): the driver made sure there were enough stops and starts to make us fall about in the back before taking us to an empty hall to sleep on a bare floor.

Our first breakfast was eggs and porridge slopped onto shaped metal trays called *varkpanne* (pig pans). It was surprisingly edible. Then came our formal induction into the unit: interviews, documentation, haircut (very short) and the issuing of uniforms, bedding, a metal trunk known as a *trommel*, a rifle and other equipment. Then we were sent scurrying with it all to our allocated *kaserne* (barracks), which for some reason were called 'bungalows' in English even though there was nothing remotely resort-like about them.

Everything was done on the double, with orders issued in fluent Afrikaans or broken English, peppered with curses. We learned to fear and obey everyone, irrespective of rank. Corporals were our undisputed leaders; officers were like gods. Everyone seemed angry and yelled at the slightest provocation. It was hell.

That evening we were given a lecture on how to shave, brush our teeth and use toilet paper. The need for these lessons became clear the next morning, when we found a pile of paper unrolled on the bathroom floor. A screaming corporal quickly got to the bottom of the story. A farm boy had sought out the hard centre of the toilet roll in lieu of the corncobs he was accustomed to using. I realised that I'd had a pretty sheltered upbringing in Cape Town.

Other hygiene tips also seemed to have been in vain. A week later, I was using the urinal before lunch when I noticed the recruit next to me holding his penis and cutlery set with the same hand. A fine spray of urine dripped steadily from his fork.

I was called many names in my crowded bungalow. Mostly it was *Jood*. Another was 'communist' because I was outspoken in my disapproval of apartheid. A third was 'professor', for seeming to know something about everything. (Just enough to be dangerous, actually.)

By my name, Rob, not so much.

I'm not going to describe the physical challenges of basic

training other than to say it was an intensive three-month pro-gramme to change raw civilians into obedient soldiers by scaring the crap out of them. After basics, soldiers would be individ-ually graded and assigned to specialist roles such as officer or non-commissioned officer (NCO), infantry, sapper or, for the lowest grade, kitchen duties.

We were often pushed to exhaustion and beyond. While show-ering one evening, I felt a sore, rough spot on my side. I scratched at it and a long thorn slid out of my flesh. I had no memory of it going in.

One evening, after a long, hot day in the bush, we were shown a training movie on how to trick and kill an enemy sniper by holding up a decoy head on a stick. Our own heads felt like they were on sticks and the corporals prowled the sleepy ranks to keep everyone awake. I was fighting a losing battle to keep my eyes open when – bam! – I saw stars as my head was slammed from behind. '*Bly wakker, Jood*' (Stay awake, Jew) the corporal warned me as he moved on to his next victim.

At other times, it was not unusual to have the Jewish recruits pulled out of the ranks to do unpleasant, menial tasks such as unloading ammunition boxes. '*Fokken Jood*' was spat at me in con-tempt several times a day. This daily verbal abuse continued until I left the air force four and a half years later. I never made an issue of it unless it became more than just harmless name-calling. Then I either fought back hard or ran away and hid.

Four weeks into basic training, I was suddenly sent, on the double, to report to the admin office. I thought I was being singled out for another lousy job, but instead I was handed a railway voucher and told to report to the Military Medical Institute in Pretoria for testing to see if I qualified for flying training. Five other recruits joined me, all of us enjoying the bliss of being allowed to snooze undisturbed in our bunks and to eat in the train's dining car – our first meal in a month not served up in a *varkpan.* We were all confident of passing the tests, but afterwards I never saw the other five again.

I was later told that of the 2 500 pilot applicants that year, about 250 were invited to Pretoria for the tests. Of these, 60 trainees were accepted for Course 2/75, scheduled to begin in June 1975 at the SAAF's Central Flying School, at Dunnottar on the East Rand. Only 34 of us would finally achieve our wings – just 1.4 per cent of those who initially applied.

Chapter 2
'You are Nothing'

Pretoria was intense. At our dimly lit orientation lecture the night before our tests started, I mistakenly referred to our blue chairs as green in a question to an officer. 'Yes,' said the officer to much laughter, 'we're going to be seeing red, green and yellow chairs in the next few days.' Clearly, the other applicants were very happy that my apparent colour-blindness improved their own odds of success.

The next morning wasn't much of an improvement. It began with the drawing of six test tubes of blood, after which I was given a thick glucose drink to compensate for the blood loss. It wasn't enough to stop me feeling light-headed as I walked away. I woke up on the floor with a bump on my head and a circle of spinning faces leaning over me. A sympathetic medic propped me up against a wall, and I sat alone in my misery.

The rest of the testing involved being bussed daily from our tent city to the Military Medical Institute, where we'd wait in line for one exam or another. We had physicals, X-rays, EEGs, EKGs and psychological screenings. Our IQs were checked along with our balance, orientation, logic and judgement skills. During the dental exam, the nurse slid a flat metal plate into my mouth to take flash pictures of my teeth and palate. When I asked why, she replied, 'That's often all that's left after a crash.' I later had several unhappy occasions to confirm that she was correct.

At last came our final interview, which I finished resplendent in my ill-fitting army tunic. I had no idea whether I'd made the grade. I suspected not, especially as my questioners seemed particularly interested in whether I planned to use my air force training as merely a stepping-stone to get into South African Airways, the national airline. I denied the thought had ever occurred to me, but I was sure they'd seen right through me.

At least I'd had a break from basic training.

I returned to Kroonstad and a fresh hell. The officers and corporals mocked me mercilessly ('useless *Jood*') because they assumed my return meant I'd already been rejected by the air force. I kept my head down and focused on finishing basics. Luckily, I got to make up for the time I'd missed by being sent off to the firing range with the weakest and sickest roofies, who were given endless rounds of ammunition and extra time to improve their aim. It was shooting heaven.

I not only became quite a good shot, but was also stunned by how strong I'd become during the training. The rifle that had felt like a lump of lead now felt like a feather, and I could run for miles without tiring. My 17-year-old body was in its best shape ever and I began to feel that I'd left boyhood behind.

I hadn't, unfortunately, left the army. With still no word from the air force by the time we had our passing-out parade, my next deployment was to an engineers' base in the Free State town of Bethlehem. I was assigned to the kitchen as a lowly cook because I'd refused to express any preference for my next posting when a panel of army officers had interviewed us individually about our interests. 'I'm going to the SAAF,' I insisted.

In Bethlehem, the portly NCO in charge of the base kitchen was delighted to see me. 'It's always lucky to have a Jew in the kitchen,' he told me. 'When you go home,' he added, 'bring me some Jewish fish and biscuits.' I assumed he meant chopped herring and sweet *kichel* crackers, a staple of South African Jewish holidays. Then he sent me to the walk-in fridge to skim the cream off several 90-litre cans of milk for him to drink.

'You are Nothing'

After a few weeks of this I finally went home for my belated passing-out leave. I was camping with friends on the scenic Berg River, about an hour from Cape Town, when I saw my father's car unexpectedly pull up to our fish braai. 'The army called,' he said. 'The air force wants to know if you still want to join the flying course.'

It was a typical army screw-up. The air force had signalled my acceptance to the Kroonstad base more than a month earlier. The army had ignored it because I'd already transferred to Bethlehem. Luckily, they were more responsive to a second signal, sent the day before the course was to begin, and called my home in Cape Town.

Camping and barbecue immediately abandoned, I was back on a train to Pretoria the next morning. By the time I got to Dunnottar, I was almost a week behind the other trainees.

Thanks to the army's poor communications, I was the last pupil pilot (pupe) to arrive at Dunnottar for Course 2/75. A curt air force corporal met me at Pretoria railway station to take me to the base. But first I was taken to Air Force Headquarters to be sworn in to the Permanent Force (career military – sorry, Herzlia teachers). There, I exchanged my baggy army browns and beret for a trim, blue air force uniform and peaked cap. I was given the white shoulder tabs and cap band of a candidate officer, the rank I would hold throughout flying training. The corporal then went to the NCOs' mess for lunch, and out of habit I went to the enlisted mess hall, where my newly acquired rank caused consternation and resentment among the airmen there.

After a long drive, I reached Dunnottar, where the adjutant informed me that there'd be an exam the next morning on aero engines. The other pupes had been studying for it all of the week I'd missed. Would I like to attempt it? Yes, I would. The distinctive snarl of Harvard radial engines kept interrupting our conversation. I felt a potent mix of excitement and trepidation as I took the dozens of thick textbooks and other course materials issued to me to my allotted bungalow. I would be sharing with 15 other pupil pilots. Being the last to arrive, I naturally got the worst bunk.

I met the senior pupes from Course 1/75, the class ahead of ours, in the bar before dinner that evening. Wise now to military ways, I stood at attention, addressed them as 'candidate officer' – even though we shared the same rank – and respectfully explained why I had arrived late. They wished me luck. I found out later that they agreed among themselves that I wouldn't last long.

The pupes were a mixed lot. Surprisingly, not all were fresh national servicemen. Some had almost completed their two-year service or were already Permanent Force members. A large percentage of our course had applied more than once for the flying programme. An older group came directly from civilian life and were known as the 'civvies'. Some had problems readjusting to military discipline, and everyone complained incessantly about the food – which was fantastic compared to the army. The oldest civvy was 25, well above the course's average age of 20. I was still only 17.

Pupes had their own mess hall and bar. There was no restriction on drinking, which turned out to be a sort of honeytrap because those who chose to drink in the evenings instead of studying were soon removed from the course. Our instructors made it crystal clear that their intent was to 'wash' each and every pupe from the programme. They weren't joking; not until we finished our wings check 18 months later could any pupe be sure they'd actually passed.

We had to write 19 exams in six weeks of ground school before they'd let us get near an aircraft. The exam pass mark was 60 per cent. Fail any three exams and you were washed. In fact, achieve a marginal pass on any three and you were out. I passed that first engines exam with 63 per cent and made sure I never got low marks again.

Unfortunately, I had to hide twice in the first month from Afrikaner pupes whose poor scores and latent anti-Semitism exploded into an urge to beat me up when they got drunk. There was no point in trying to retaliate. They were huge specimens and were on their way out anyway.

Our formal welcoming ceremony came during my second week. We were marched into the base hall, where the commanding officer (CO), a spindly fellow with a fixed smile and the swollen nose of a heavy drinker, praised us as 'the cream of South African youth' and 'the best the country has to offer'. We liked that kind of talk. Then he left and the colonel in charge of the flying school stood up.

'You are nothing,' he spat at us. 'Worthless pupes until you prove yourselves. The whole base is watching you and waiting for you to screw up. And we'll know whatever you're getting up to.'

Apparently not. Many of the English-speaking pupes had gone to boarding school and were wise in the ways of cheating. Within a few weeks, they'd bribed an admin private with beer and cash to allow them a quick glance at the discarded master copy of exam papers freshly printed on the base Roneo machine.

When the private was transferred, they raided the ground school office at night through a window they'd left a bit open for the purpose. Exam papers were securely locked in the bottom drawer of a desk, but the wily boarding-school boys simply removed the drawer above it. Then they proceeded to memorise most of the questions. Ground school wasn't such a problem after that.

But the colonel wasn't wrong on one point. The whole base was watching us. I became aware of a smouldering resentment towards pilots from non-flyers. This never quite went away, not even at SAA, where pilots were seen by ground staff as spoiled, overpaid and on permanent holiday. Eventually, I just accepted the resentment and ignored it, like every other pilot does.

Finally, we were ready to get airborne. We were warned to wear only cotton underwear and socks as a fire would melt anything made of nylon into our skin. We were ordered to remove any jewellery that could catch or strangle us if we had to bail out. And we were issued gear that included a hard helmet with a retractable dark visor and blue canvas inner headpiece with earphones, soft leather flying gloves and a parachute and harness that doubled as a seat in the Harvard. There were also several washed-out orange Nomex flying overalls, permanently stained with years of pupe perspiration. It would be years before I realised it was possible to fly without breaking into a profuse sweat.

Our first training aircraft was a single-engine Harvard,
also known as a North American Aviation T-6 Texan.

An instructor stood beside me on the wing when I eventually strapped myself nervously into the Harvard cockpit for my first engine start. All of the SAAF's Harvards had been grounded shortly before we were due to start flying because a wing had broken clean off a Harvard, pulling out of a practice bombing dive. The unlucky Citizen Force (CF) pilot – the CF were the part-time or reserve forces – was mashed into a 'fetch the teeth photos' mess; we were assigned to practise the starts and Vital Actions (VAs, or memorised checklist items) while the rest of our Harvards were inspected for wing cracks.

I finished the pre-start procedures, primed the engine and pressed the starter. The prop swung and caught with a roar. In my excitement, I managed to knock the park brake off. The aircraft had just been rolled into position and chocks hadn't been placed in front of the wheels. Without chocks and with too much throttle, the Harvard hopped over the grass verge and began moving briskly along the hard apron towards other parked machines. I discovered that the 'rumour' we'd shared was true. When the Harvard's big radial engine fired, all your hard-learned lessons indeed disappeared from your head. I stared blankly at the whirling disc of the propellor while the windswept instructor, holding on for dear life, screamed, 'The brakes, Schapiro, hit the fucking brakes.' Sanity returned and I closed the throttle and pressed the toe brakes on top of the rudders. The plane ground to a halt and the instructor staggered off the wing to find chocks. The incident deeply amused the other instructors, who told me I should log two minutes' taxi time.

Like most pupes, I wasn't a natural pilot. It took time, repetition and lots of effort to develop the skills and muscle memory of a competent aviator. Military pilots have to learn to function in an environment full of distractions. The Harvard cockpit is not a quiet place. The radial engine is extremely loud, the radio blares and everything vibrates. It's often hot and it always stinks of fuel and oil. It's definitely not conducive to clear thinking and it takes a while to learn to function well under such conditions. Some pupes never did. Although they excelled in a quiet classroom, they constantly forgot things in the hot, noisy cockpit environment. In military flight training, you were expected to have made sufficient progress after a specified number of flight hours to pass a progress check. If you didn't make the grade, you weren't given extra time to improve – you were washed. Their attitude was that you might make a fine pilot, but it wouldn't be in the air force.

Many pupes' flying careers were cut short by over-aggressive instructors or poor-quality instruction in their *ab initio* (from the beginning) training. Luckily, I had the good fortune to be assigned to a wonderful *ab initio* instructor – a patient, soft-spoken ex-chopper pilot with a friendly wife and a ten-kilogram cat. I was often given the job of feeding the cat.

My training captain's patience wasn't unlimited. There were many occasions when I'd find myself panting to the distant AGA (Aerodrome Ground Aid) homing beacon and back with my heavy parachute slung over my shoulder – a well-trodden punishment run by many generations of pupes. He was particularly pissed off when I taxied a Harvard into a meerkat hole and had to be towed out backwards, with smirking senior staff watching the whole debacle.

But he was also there to help me when I struggled to find the correct round-out (flare) height – when the pilot raises the aircraft nose to soften touchdown. I would fly the Harvard into the ground and it would bounce wildly back into the air. Or I would round out too high and float down the runway. In desperation, he ordered me to climb onto the roof of the toilet block, which happened to be at the correct flare height, and to sit there for a couple of hours while pretending I was landing. It worked.

There were other major milestones. One morning, we were droning around the circuit doing touch-and-go landings. I was doing reasonably well when halfway through the hour, the captain ordered me to make the next one a full stop and to taxi to the dispersal area (parking apron). I thought I'd screwed something up again, but after I parked, he told me to keep the engine running and hopped out. He leaned into the cockpit: 'Give me one circuit and full stop landing, Schapiro.' Then he made his way to the control tower without looking back.

I waited in the idling Harvard while ground crew ran for the log and authorisation books and brought them to the aircraft.

'You are Nothing'

I signed out an aircraft for my very first time, hardly believing this was happening to me. I definitely didn't feel ready.

My 'first solo flight' certificate

I taxied out slowly, did my pre-takeoff checks and was about to line up on the grass runway, when the captain yelled from the tower that I'd forgotten to do a power check. I cursed myself, did the belated power check and then lined up. The circuit had been completely cleared for a first solo, so I opened the throttle and accelerated down the runway. The Harvard took smoothly to the air. Everything felt exactly the same as before, until I joined the downwind circuit and turned my head to scan for other traffic. I instantly saw that the seat behind me was empty, its seatbelt neatly coupled together. I was in the air alone! A great thrill surged over me, but I still had to get the machine back on the ground. I calmed down and concentrated on making a nice approach and landing. All too soon, and with a small bounce, I was back on the ground. I taxied in, enormously pleased with myself.

Cheering pupes carried me from the aircraft and treated me to the traditional mudbath while the instructors watched the spectacle from open windows. 'Schapiro, you are the third Jew to ever solo here,' one called out. Who were the other two, I wondered.

The next big test was a solo spin and recovery. A spin is when an aircraft ceases to fly and plunges uncontrollably towards the earth in a tight spiral. We had to demonstrate that we could perform the special technique to recover from it before we smacked into the ground.

For some reason, the exercise was always carried out over the Union Carriage & Wagon factory, a huge railway wagon assembly plant close to the airfield. I'm sure their workers would not have appreciated knowing that training aircraft were plunging earthwards towards them on a daily basis.

The exercise went off fine, although being somewhat nervous about spinning, I recovered after just one rotation instead of the required three. No one seemed to notice or care, least of all me.

I started to do solo aerobatics. As I headed out to the General Flying Area to practise manoeuvres, I looked down at the cars on the roads and thought how strange it was that I wasn't allowed to drive a car yet. At 17, I still wasn't old enough to get a driver's licence.

Chapter 3
Weapons and Wings

Our Harvard phase ended in 1976, after we had soloed, learned aerobatics, performed cross-country navigation and done some instrument flying. Class 2/75 was then transferred to Impala jet training at Langebaanweg Air Force Base (AFB) to add night flying, low-level navigation, formation flying and advanced instrument flying to our repertoire – provided we could keep passing the progress checks.

I drove the two hours to Langebaanweg from our family home in Cape Town in my first car, a 1960s red Triumph Spitfire coupé. The first thing I noticed as I entered the base was the intoxicating smell of burnt jet fuel, so different from the gasoline used by piston-engine machines. Then a familiar car pulled up behind me, tooting its horn. It was my father. I'd left my uniform jacket and cap in Cape Town and he and a friend had driven all the way to Langebaanweg to bring them to me. I was still a *loskop*!

After the predictable hazing by senior pupes, we settled down to learn how to fly the MB-326 Impala, an Italian-designed jet trainer built in South Africa. Jets are easier to fly than propeller-driven planes but everything happens much more quickly. Just the takeoff speed of the Impala was faster than we'd ever managed to fly in Harvards.

Yet again I had the good fortune of having an excellent instructor. This captain was a handsome, dark-haired man of German descent with a foul mouth and precise standards.

'Schapiro, what's your climb speed now?' he might ask in flight.

'219 knots, Captain.'

'What should it be, Schapiro?'

'220, Captain.'

'So fucking fix it!'

Unfortunately, he was so good he was often assigned to help struggling pupes, and I then got the lousy instructor who probably caused their problems in the first place.

There was other training too. The corporal who took care of our drill and fitness at Langebaanweg was called Wollies. An Afrikaans-speaker, he'd often yell at us in broken English: 'Where is your proud?' (meaning pride, I guess).

One day he wanted to punish a few of us for something or other, so he loaded us into a Bedford truck and drove about 25 kilometres along a pitted dirt road next to a railway line. 'Now run back, you *bliksems* (bastards),' Wollies ordered as he turned the Bedford around in a cloud of dust.

We set off at a listless pace in the stinging heat. Before long we heard the chuffing of a locomotive coming down the track. One of us, a former part-time fireman on steam locomotives in Johannesburg, knew the routine to flag down the freight train. After a few words with the engineer, we all clambered into an open freight car.

The train almost beat Wollies' Bedford back to camp. We waited him out by relaxing in a nearby café, then soaked ourselves with water and ran 'exhausted' into the camp, witnessed by a triumphant Wollies.

On the flying front, I was already solid enough to survive some bad instruction, but I still had a few scary solo incidents during this training period. On one occasion I got distracted during a flapless landing exercise, allowing the speed to decay slightly on final approach. That's a bad thing to do without lift-generating flaps. Suddenly I felt the stick shudder, a warning of an imminent stall. I recovered by jamming on the thrust, but it was close. A few knots lower and the Impala would have stalled at an unrecoverable altitude.

Weapons and Wings

The second stage of our training was learning to fly the MB-326 Impala jet.

Worse was when the jet in front of me decided to do an unannounced full stop landing while I was doing touch-and-go circuits and landings. As I already had landing clearance and didn't know any better, I continued the approach and landed even though he was still taxiing on the runway. The pilot had moved over to the right of the centreline, so I moved to the left, flashed by him at high speed and took off again. Air traffic control said nothing, and only years later did I realise how incredibly dangerous and stupid it was to land with him on the runway.

My worst Impala incident happened on a night-time cross-country navigation exercise. Halfway into the solo flight, I estimated that I should be over a particular small town even though I couldn't see its lights. No problem in an aerobatic jet: I flipped the Impala onto its back, saw the town directly below and flipped upright again. But the violent manoeuvre produced a strong surge of vertigo and now the ground lights seemed to merge with the stars to create a false horizon. I battled to resist the intense feeling that the jet was in a steep bank despite the instruments showing my Impala upright and level. The vertigo gradually faded and my pounding heart returned to normal. I had given myself a serious fright and vowed never to do anything stupid like that again.

Others weren't as lucky. Military flying is inherently dangerous and military training even more so. The aircraft are high-performance machines and young, aggressive pilots often take risks. The career of one of my best friends came to an early end when he and his instructor were forced to eject after an imbalance in the wingtip fuel tanks made a spin manoeuvre unrecoverable. The rocket pack beneath the ejector seat blasted them out of the cockpit and the parachute behind the seat got them onto the ground. The problem is that this blast is so powerful it invariably damages a pilot's back.

I visited my friend in military hospital a few days after the incident. He was drifting in and out of consciousness, muttering incoherently. He'd been knocked out when his head went through the plane's Perspex canopy and part of his chin was scraped off when he hit the ground. I noticed that his ears were still full of soil. Doctors sewed up his chin and cleaned out his ears, but he never returned to flying.

Eventually, it was time for our final tests.

My navigation check was taken by none other than my former instructor, the dark-haired captain with the precise standards. It was against the rules for an instructor to check his own pupe, but by then this captain had moved around so much that no one made the connection. I certainly wasn't complaining.

The check involved three different disciplines: medium-, low- and high-level navigation. The medium-level sector went well. I flew to Bloemfontein, did the required approach and landing, then took a short break while the Impala was refuelled. I knew that the low-level navigation – flying at 200 feet above ground level (AGL) – would be much trickier. I found the start point and carefully set my heading for the exercise. I doubt I knew where I was more than half the time, but luckily I'd had a tip from a senior pupe that the end point lay exactly behind a radio mast visible from more than 40 miles out. When I spotted a tall, thin tower in the distance I took a chance and made a slight course correction towards it. I breathed a sigh of relief when I flew right over the final fix. Captain Precise was so impressed by my 'skill' that I got a top score for navigation – and he flew most of the high-level sector back to Langebaanweg himself.

One new hurdle still had to be cleared before our wings parade.

The powers that be had decided Course 2/75 needed to complete a short weapons course. We'd learned how to fly the jet; we would now learn how to use it as a weapon using 0.50 Browning machine guns, 78-mm rockets and 12.5-kg practice bombs.

The mission profile was invariably the same. With an instructor in the back seat, we'd taxi out and line up in formation on the runway. Waiting armourers would scamper between the jets to arm the weapons. We'd place our hands on our helmets to reassure them that our fingers were far away from the trigger. Then we'd take off and fly in loose formation to the range, check in with the range controller and join the circuit. In sequence we'd dive towards the target, release or fire the weapons, pull out and repeat the exercise until empty, and then return to base individually.

I knew the area pretty well. The range was situated on a small, windswept peninsula that jutted into the cold Atlantic Ocean; the entire area was part of a designated nature reserve. I'd once volunteered to spend a day at the desolate range between my training missions, spotting shots for other pilots. We trucked out before dawn to be in position for the first flight of the day. It was a hot, thankless job. I was stuck by myself in one of three airless concrete bunkers with a direction finder and radio to triangulate the fall of missiles or bombs.

While I sweated it out, our small wiry sergeant – quite

Secrets from the Cockpit

Getting my wings from Lieutenant General Bob Rogers,
Chief of the South African Air Force

indifferent to the reserve status of the range – went out at midday with his rifle and shot a small buck in the head for his lunch. He immediately gutted it and fried the liver in a large lump of fat he'd brought along for the purpose. He then added a crayfish he'd poached earlier that morning. He didn't offer to share. The rest of us ate dry sandwiches from the mess for lunch.

We didn't use rifles on that pre-wings weapons course. First up were machine guns. With a 0.50 Browning under each wing, I dove towards the target, passed the 'commence firing' line and pulled the trigger. The jet vibrated and twin lines of ground impacts marched towards the target. It looked amazing, just like in the movies!

Unlike in the movies, many of my rounds missed the target and I got a mediocre passing score for gunnery.

Next up were rockets. We'd dive in, pull the trigger and a smoky trail would blast out ahead, quickly dropping below the nose of the jet. I actually achieved a 'Coke' (bullseye) with one round and passed rockets handsomely.

Finally, we dropped bombs. This is where things went wrong for me. The problem was that the bombs were released by pushing a button on top of the joystick – not by pulling the trigger, as we'd done for the rockets and guns. It didn't help that I had an excitable twerp for an instructor that day. I made my first bombing dive, lined up nicely and pulled the trigger instead of pushing the button.

'No bomb,' the range spotters announced as I pulled out of the dive. 'What happened?' the instructor asked. 'I pulled the trigger by mistake,' I admitted.

We went around again and dived in. Incredibly, I made the same mistake. This time the instructor erupted wildly, screaming at me and thumping the canopy with his fists. I turned the earphone volume right down but I could still hear him yelling and thumping. Somewhat distracted by the ongoing mayhem in the back seat, I made a third attempt. Unbelievably, I pulled the trigger again! I realised what I had done the moment I did it and pressed the release button anyway as I was pulling out. The practice bomb came off the bomb rack and was tossed a mile beyond the range. It exploded in dry brush and instantly started a smoky fire that quickly obscured the range.

'Range is closed,' the spotters announced as civilian fire engines raced in to deal with the spreading veld fire. I flew back in disgrace.

Luckily, my final wings test was largely uneventful. I walked out to the jet as a dumb pupe and returned as a military pilot. After 18 months of unrelenting tension and effort, I was too numb to celebrate – that would come later.

Chapter 4
Officers and Gentlemen

Our wings parade was held at Dunnottar, where we'd begun our training those long months before. It was a grand affair: 34 sets of wings were pinned on 34 tunics by the Chief of the Air Force while a formation of Harvards flew noisily overhead and our families watched proudly from the audience. My parents were among those flown in by the air force on a four-engine C-130 Hercules transport. Predictably, my mother got airsick on the flight, but she was there with everyone else to celebrate our achievement. There might have been less celebration if these relatives knew how many of us would die in the next few years.

That evening there was a formal dinner dance at the officers' club. Girlfriends and dates were asked to bring along a needle and thread to take part in an air force tradition – sewing the freshly awarded wings onto our tunics. I invited a sweet girl I'd met at a party and she bought an expensive new dress for the event.

I went with a friend in his large Chrysler sedan to pick up our dates. The car was a replacement for his late Volkswagen Beetle, which had once memorably seized up when he forgot to put in oil before driving us to a small game reserve in Mkuze in Natal (today KwaZulu-Natal). That time, we'd ended up marooned in a remote rural area without a telephone. This time, he managed to hit a kerb and burst a front tyre. (Yes, I admit we'd had one or two drinks by then.) Naturally, the spare tyre was also flat, so we got to my date's house an hour late. Her mother answered the door, her lips tightly pursed, and it went downhill from there. Suffice to say I went to the dance alone and my friend's girlfriend sewed my wings on. I have to say that she sewed better than he drove.

Earning our wings hadn't made us officers or gentlemen. We were sent to correct that at a three-month officers' course at the SAAF College in Pretoria. But first, six of us decided to properly celebrate our success with a long-overdue boozy weekend. We hired a large caravan, filled our vehicles with cases of beer, boxes of wine and a few cans of beans and headed off to a campground in the Northern Transvaal. We arrived after dark, paid for the weekend and were directed to an open space to set up our camp. The owners spent the next two days trying to get us to leave.

Our behaviour was disgraceful. To avoid problems with the SAAF, we claimed to be railway labourers. We were so drunk and loud that other campers refused to park near us. Arguments flared when irate parents and husbands came to extract daughters and wives attracted to our site by our music and bad-boy aura. The lone family that stayed within our evacuated zone spent the weekend quietly finishing their giant-sized plastic drum of homemade red wine. By the second day, we sent out for more beer. Everyone breathed a sigh of relief when we left.

Officer training wasn't like the pupes' course at all. I shared my small bungalow with the friend who'd cost me my post-parade date; we were woken in the morning with hot coffee and buttered toast. Our shoes were shined overnight to a soft gloss, beds were made daily and our laundry was washed and ironed once a week.

Officers' inspection took place every Friday morning. We'd tidy our room, then stand ready in our half blues – no tunics needed – and flying jackets. One Friday, my roommate surprised me by running outside when we heard the inspecting officer entering the bungalow next door. I was confused until I heard a noise on my window and turned to look. A yellow stream was hosing onto my spotless glass! My roommate finished peeing and ran back inside, laughing. The officer entered, looked around and rebuked me for my dripping, yellow mess of a window. I hid my anger and pretended to my roommate that I was amused by his prank. Then I worked on my revenge.

That Sunday evening, I waited patiently until my roommate was washing his hair in the shower, then ran in and did to him what he had done to my window. He screamed and tried to run away from the hot stream, but his eyes were so full of stinging shampoo that he made my watering job easier by running in little circles. I don't think I wasted a single drop.

Weekends were wild. We'd head into Pretoria to drink and party. Our favourite hangouts were the German Club for beer and schnapps or a large beer hall to meet girls. Once a guy at the beer hall came from behind and threw me to the floor. I don't remember exactly why, but I think it had something to do with my kissing his attractive girlfriend.

When we weren't partying, there was work to be done. Classes included military science, business and management principles – and a heavy dose of vile government propaganda. I found the academic material interesting, but I was so annoyed by the blatant, childish racist politics and so disappointed to hear such rhetoric from educated officers that – somewhat imprudently – I spoke out against it. Once again, I was called a communist. I certainly wasn't a communist, but in South Africa the label was regularly pinned on anyone who spoke out against apartheid. I later wondered if I'd gone too far with my big mouth and might fail the course, but I ended up doing surprisingly well.

In our last week of the officers' course, we were taken on a five-day hike through the majestic Blyde River Canyon in the Eastern Transvaal.

We didn't get to enjoy the scenery at all. Each day we had to complete increasingly tough navigation exercises and hump our backpacks, stuffed with a week's food and water, up and down steep hills. We became progressively more exhausted and were quickly sweating out all the beer we'd swilled on the weekends. I also learned that going down a hill is much harder on the legs than going up. The last day was the worst. Already close to exhaustion, we climbed a hill so steep that we could lean forward and touch the ground. But at the top were a couple of welcoming Bedfords, a smoking braai, salads and urns of tea. Officers' course was over.

My screw-up on the weapons course meant I wasn't selected to fly fighter jets. Instead, 1977 saw me as one of the six newly minted pilot officers from Course 2/75 to get posted to multi-engine training school in Bloemfontein to learn to fly C-47 Dakotas. As they didn't carry bombs, it suited me just fine.

Flying in the SAAF (left). After getting my wings, I was sent to learn to fly C-47 Dakotas (right).

Unlike Pretoria, weekends were quiet and lonely in Bloemfontein. The capital of the Orange Free State (now Free State) was a sleepy city during the week, shut down on Saturday afternoon and comatose on Sunday. I took to going to synagogue on Friday nights for conversation, company and the family meal I was invariably invited to after the service. One such dinner was with a pleasant couple and their two sons, home for the weekend from their own army service. Unfortunately, they, like so many other Jewish conscripts, were incredulous that I'd signed on for the Permanent

Force. To the dismay of their parents, they mocked me throughout the meal. I ate, left and never went back to Friday-night services again.

Luckily, I had the flying to keep me busy. The C-47 was a military adaptation of the Douglas DC-3 built for commercial airlines back in the 1930s. A twin radial-engine transport aircraft, it remained in use for decades after World War II because of its amazing versatility and rugged construction. But it was a beast to learn to fly. Heavy manual controls, a taildragger configuration and a pre-takeoff VAs checklist that stretched on for pages demanded full attention and skill to master.

My first familiarisation flight didn't go well. Scheduled to last an hour, it took me 45 minutes to complete the Before Start, After Start, Taxi, Power Check and Before Takeoff checks. That left only 15 minutes to fly, land, taxi in and shut down. No one else did any better. We were warned to pick it up or fail.

I spent hours after class practising these VAs, using my hands to reach for imaginary controls, levers or switches – a practice I later continued with printed paper panels every time I moved to a new aircraft. Finally, I got the time for the pre-takeoff VAs down to less than seven minutes, leaving me free to concentrate on learning to handle the C-47 on the ground and in the air.

Ground operations were a constant challenge, especially in high winds. On taildragger planes the two main wheels of the landing gear are situated forward of the centre of gravity; a small wheel supports the tail. Taildraggers are steered from behind in a way that's been compared to driving a car backwards at high speed. That made taxiing a Dakota almost an art form, needing a delicate touch and perfect technique to avoid ground-looping (spinning around) or damaging the huge fabric rudder by allowing wind to flap it over wildly.

Short takeoffs and landings with the big machine had their own drama.

Unlike the regular smooth takeoff procedure, we lowered half flaps and applied full power against brakes, then suddenly released them. The tail came up instantly as the plane leaped forward and we dragged the Dakota into the air at an incredibly low speed. On the first short-takeoff demonstration, I stared out the side window and marvelled out loud at the steep climb angle. 'Fuck the view, Schapiro, look at the instruments,' my instructor fumed.

Landing a huge taildragger had other challenges. While practising crosswind landings, where the wind isn't directly down the runway, I allowed the wind to swing the tail and was slow to react. The C-47 began to slew sideways, and only swift, firm action from my instructor prevented a disaster. The lesson was clear: you correct a tail swing immediately, almost before it happens, or it's too late.

Then there were the leaks. We'd noticed on our first day in the hangars that all of the Daks had flat metal pans placed under their engines. Most of the pans held puddles of black, viscous oil that was visibly dripping from the engine cowls. When we politely asked the hangar sergeant major about the leaks, he grumbled that if a Dakota engine wasn't leaking oil 'it doesn't have any'.

Later we were puzzled by an instruction to cover all our aviation charts with plastic folio (wrap). This went against normal protocol of replacing old charts rather than trying to preserve them. Our confusion ended when we flew into a rainstorm. The Dakota cockpit and windscreen leaked like a sieve and water dripped on us from everywhere. The plastic-covered maps doubled as raincoats to keep the water off.

Other issues were harder to protect ourselves from. The C-47 was an unpressurised aircraft, which meant we avoided operating above 11 000 feet because higher altitudes required supplementary oxygen. Against my better judgement I once flew a navigator-school night exercise with a streaming cold. While descending into Ysterplaat AFB from high altitude, an excruciating sinus pain began behind my eyes. The feeling that needles were being pushed into my brain left me barely able to concentrate on flying.

I vowed never to repeat the experience, but my sinus problems continued for most of my flying career – and ultimately played a role in ending it 32 years later.

Chapter 5
Sex, Politics and Near Misses

Fuck. We were about to go into the ocean without anyone even knowing we had a problem.

It was a fine Cape Town morning. I was in a Dakota in the designated General Flying Area off the Atlantic coastline on our monthly instrument-flying training session. One of the required exercises was to fly with an engine out. At 6 500 feet I asked my co-pilot, JIT – a nickname derived from the initials of his first three names, Jan Izak Tobias – to cut off the fuel mixture to one of the engines. He pulled back a fuel lever and I went into the shutdown and feathering procedure for that engine.

Except that the propeller wouldn't feather.

After a second futile attempt I gave up and ordered JIT to put the fuel mixture back in. But the engine wouldn't take power back either.

This was a major problem. A C-47 can fly perfectly well on one engine – provided the other is feathered with its blades turned 90 degrees into the airstream to minimise drag. Our engine was windmilling, which meant it was turning in the airstream without power and creating too much drag for the remaining engine to maintain altitude. I'd have to descend to maintain flying speed. JIT, a good friend, was swearing and trying to troubleshoot the problem.

Meanwhile we were descending steadily, still heading out to sea. I turned the Dakota back towards Ysterplaat and opened METO (maximum except takeoff) power on the good engine to try and reduce our sink rate. It barely helped. I felt a surge of anxiety as it dawned on me that at our current sink rate, we couldn't make it back to Ysterplaat. JIT continued to fiddle fruitlessly with the unresponsive engine.

Could we make it to Robben Island, I wondered? No, it would be too dangerous to try. The airstrip there was too short for a single-engine landing and we might crash into the icy ocean just short of the island. The only thing left to do was a controlled ditching off the beaches of Camps Bay and to swim ashore. The problem: we'd lazily dropped our inflatable life vests in the back when we'd got into the plane. It was too late to retrieve them.

'Call Cape Town ATC,' I ordered JIT, who had by then given up on the windmilling engine. 'Tell them we have engine trouble and must ditch off Camps Bay.' He tried to raise Cape Town on the radio but we'd already dropped below the level of the surrounding mountains. This blocked our transmissions to the airport and there was no response from air traffic control. If we hit the water, no one would know.

As we turned towards Camps Bay to ditch the C-47 behind the big waves off the beach, I told JIT to release and eject the cockpit-roof escape hatch. When he stood to do so, I heard a change in engine tone. I glanced down at the engine instruments and saw that, for some reason, the windmilling engine had dropped from its 1 500 rpm to 1 200 rpm. I nudged the throttle and the engine responded! I pushed the throttle wide open and the engine took full power and we climbed away.

We'd been less than 300 feet from the water.

We were dead quiet in the cockpit on the flight back to base. We landed, taxied to the hangars and shut down. I reported what had happened to the hangar sergeant major. 'Not possible, Lieutenant,' he advised. 'You must have screwed something up. An engine either feathers or takes power.' I felt JIT and I needed to get back into the air quickly. We were still shaking from our close call and needed to fly in order to get over it. I asked the sergeant major to come with us on a test flight to see if we could replicate the problem. He reluctantly agreed.

We took off and climbed to 7 000 feet directly over the airfield. The sceptical mechanic stood between us observing as the co-pilot pulled the fuel mixture lever and tried to feather the engine. It immediately went into the same unresponsive condition. 'There you are, Sergeant Major, fix it,' I yelled over the engine noise. He leaned forward with a furrowed brow and began manipulating the engine controls. The furrows deepened as nothing helped.

We flew in wide, easy circles as we descended steadily over the base. As I set up for a high downwind landing, the sweating sergeant major became increasingly frantic in his troubleshooting efforts. We landed with only one engine working; the bad one never came back at all.

JIT and I had quite a few drinks that evening, but his luck ran out a few years later. On 14 July 1982 he was the captain of a 21 Squadron Swearingen Merlin IVA that was returning from South West Africa to Pretoria. He was descending to land at Waterkloof AFB when his aircraft collided with a civilian Piper Navajo that had just taken off from Lanseria. Jan Izak Tobias de Villiers died in the collision, along with two other SAAF crew members, five passengers and the four occupants of the Piper. He was 25. He left behind a wife and young child.

I was flying for 25 Squadron at the time JIT and I had our near miss. The air force had granted my request to transfer to Ysterplaat after all of us had passed our checks to qualify as multi-engine pilots. I'd been thrilled beyond words to be going home again – and to be able to enjoy the Cape's spectacular scenery from the cockpit. One gorgeous Atlantic Ocean beach we often made a point of flying over was Sandy Bay, a secluded haven for nudists – and gawkers.

Secrets from the Cockpit

One day a friend and I decided to pay the beach a ground-level visit. We stripped down and were walking around when, to our surprise, we encountered some visiting air hostess corporals from a Pretoria VIP squadron. It's tough to pull rank when you have no clothes on. The next day brought an even more sensitive problem. We'd both got severely burned in areas that didn't generally see the sun. We could barely walk and peeing was agony. We asked our CO if we could have light duties on grounds of sunburn. He looked puzzled and said we didn't look burned. We showed him. We got our time off and a lecture on proper behaviour for an officer.

It wasn't my last lecture from the commandant. While at Ysterplaat I acquired an unsuitable, older girlfriend who amused herself by giving me what she called 'night classes'. Night classes were one thing but sleeping all day in the crew room was another, so the CO again called me into his office. 'Rob,' he began, 'a man can have sex only so many times in his life. You are going to use it all up in one year. Slow down!'

I did not slow down.

Unlike modern airliners, which fly over most bad weather, the unpressurised C-47 flies right through it. I'd become used to it, but one trip was especially memorable – for more than one reason.

We were flying from Port Elizabeth to Cape Town at 8 000 feet into the teeth of a cold front that was blanketing the Cape Peninsula. As its name implies, the peninsula is surrounded on three sides by sea and blocked from the rest of the country by tall mountain ranges – a topographic barrier that can produce extreme weather conditions. In summer, the prevailing southeasterly wind creates severe turbulence as it howls at 30 to 40 knots over the mountains. But the worst weather is in the winter, when cold fronts bring heavy rain and icing. The harshest effects are at precisely the altitudes where the prop-driven Dakota flies.

Sex, Politics and Near Misses

We quickly entered solid cloud cover and before long were using our plastic-covered 'raincoat' maps to keep the cold drips off. The outside temperature dropped steadily to below freezing and the rain turned to ice, which began to build up rapidly on the windscreen. We could also see ice on the nacelles housing the engines, so we knew it was accumulating on the wings and propellers as well. The C-47 has a basic de-icing system that pumps an alcohol-laced fluid onto the windscreen or propellers. The rest of the plane is unprotected. The ice build-up started to unbalance the props and the plane began to vibrate. We gave the props a blast of alcohol and, with a loud banging, chunks of ice slid off the blades and impacted the fuselage. Suddenly the cabin-heater warning light flicked on, indicating overheating. The cold air intake was becoming choked with ice so we shut the system down. It grew freezing cold inside the Dakota.

The weight of ice packing onto the airframe was taking its toll and our cruise speed was steadily decreasing. We got clearance to climb to 10 000 feet to try get out of the icing zone. But despite full climb power, too much ice and reduced efficiency from the coated wings kept the C-47 from climbing much higher. We gained 500 feet and then it refused to climb any more, the steady roar of the engines punctuated with occasional bangs from the prop ice.

I wasn't worried yet. 'If it won't go up,' I told the co-pilot, 'we'll have to go down.' We descended slowly until we were at the minimum safety altitude (MSA) above the mountain ranges. The thick windscreen ice began to wash away and we got our raincoat maps out as the icy drips started again.

As the ice washed off the airframe, our speed gradually increased and we tried the shut-down cabin heater system. A stream of warm air blew into the freezing-cold cockpit. Yes! As we left the mountains behind us, turbulence shook off the last of the ice and we began our descent into Ysterplaat.

39

Secrets from the Cockpit

Not your regular airline trip perhaps, but a typical flight in a Dakota.

Oh yes. I turned 21 on that trip.

My unit, 25 Squadron, was a mixed-duty outfit. We flew long training flights for trainee navigators, many of whom had gone to navigation school after washing out of pilot training, and provided weekly military shuttles from Cape Town to Durban and Swartkop AFB in Pretoria. There were some special missions transporting government or military VIPs to unusual destinations and an occasional shuttle up the West Coast to Rooikop AFB (Walvis Bay) in South West Africa.

The seven-hour Rooikop flight took us over the desolate Skeleton Coast and Namib Desert. Usually, we flew the sector at 10 000 feet but sometimes we elected to do it at low level. Then we'd fly at 1 000 feet or less above the uninhabited, wild coastline, with tall desert sand dunes just a short distance inland. I noticed a disturbing phenomenon. It was sometimes impossible to visually gauge your height over the barren dunes, especially if there were no shadows. Without features such as trees, the dunes removed all frames of reference to assess your altitude and you could fly into them very easily. The same effect occurs over smooth water, snow or salt pans.

When I later went to northern South West Africa, we often flew at low levels over the Etosha National Park. This game reserve is named for a salt pan so sprawling it can be seen from space. My vantage point was far lower and sometimes I judged our height above the pan by looking at our shadow on the ground. If the shadow started coming closer, we were descending. Then I'd ease pressure off the yoke (throttle) until the shadow looked right again. I also learned to keep the aircraft trimmed slightly nose-up during low-level flying so that if we got distracted, it would tend to climb, not descend.

Sex, Politics and Near Misses

Other missions involved towing a target drogue for army anti-aircraft artillery and naval gunnery training. We often worried that the trainee gunners might target our specially marked yellow-and-black-striped Dakota, but it turned out that they rarely hit anything at all. We found it boring to fly in a fixed pattern off the coast or to do figures of eight over a warship in False Bay, but the best part of the mission was dropping the drogue. Then we'd skim low over the coast, often seeing great white sharks in the water. We agreed we'd never, ever swim there.

One of our stranger missions was to fly a dolphin from Cape Town to the Durban aquarium. A small team of marine biologists came along to tend to the captive mammal, which was brought to the aircraft on a canvas sling, covered with thick opaque grease to keep it moist. Sadly, the dolphin became so stressed during the flight that it overheated and melted the protective grease. The frantic biologists tried to cool the dolphin with water but it died in the air. Our plane landed in Durban to be met by a smiling delegation of aquarium officials waiting to welcome their new acquisition. We quickly fled the air base before they got the bad news and we got the blame for their dead dolphin.

Other memorable flights included our occasional trips to Robben Island, then home to the world's most famous political prisoner, Nelson Mandela, and many other jailed leaders of the anti-apartheid movement. Mandela would spend 18 of his 27 years in jail on the island. In true apartheid style, Robben Island was reserved for black prisoners – both political and common criminals. Mandela's white fellow activists served their sentences in Pretoria Central Prison.

I particularly remember the day a senior commander and I were ordered to fly a group of Ysterplaat airmen to the island for a sports event with the prison warders. The island's short airstrip ended abruptly, close to the Atlantic Ocean, so at least one of the pilots on board had to be experienced in short landings. The flight was chock-full of air force members and their equipment, which meant we took a reduced fuel load to facilitate the landing. We emerged from the plane and wondered what we'd do for the next few hours.

The warders were having none of it. 'If you're here, you must compete,' they insisted. We volunteered to make a darts team. Darts was a favourite 25 Squadron activity and we expected to do well against the jailers. We didn't realise that there was little else to do on the island so they played darts for hours every day. We were slaughtered.

I have no idea if we saw Mandela. During those years his photograph and statements were banned from publication, so we had no idea what he looked like. But it still intrigues me to think that he or other leaders of the struggle against apartheid may have been among the prisoners who cleared our plates and cups while we played darts with the barely literate guards.

Chapter 6
Fokker at the Border

I was first deployed to fly in South Africa's Border War in 1978. The war is named for the 1 400-kilometre border between the South African territory of South West Africa (now Namibia) and the former Portuguese colony of Angola. Since 1966, the South African Defence Force had been fighting an insurgency by guerrillas of the South West Africa People's Organisation (Swapo), who often operated from bases in Angola. After the 1974 military coup in Portugal led to Lisbon's rapid granting of independence to its remaining colonies, Angola's armed groups fought to take control of the country. The Marxist Popular Movement for the Liberation of Angola (MPLA) became the country's new government. South Africa, with tacit backing from Washington, threw its support behind one of the MPLA's rivals, the Union for the Total Independence of Angola (Unita). The conflict soon became a proxy for the wider Cold War between the United States and the Soviet Union after Cuba, backed by Moscow, intervened in support of the MPLA. The Border War was complicated, but what it boiled down to was that Pretoria wanted to prevent Swapo insurgents from infiltrating South West Africa via safe havens in Angola and to destabilise the pro-communist government in Luanda.

I did my first two tours on the border with the major who had become my mentor. A pedantic, cautious pilot, he tolerated no deviation from standard operating procedures (SOPs) and, as the squadron's official checker/instructor, demanded high standards from everyone. Many air force pilots were satisfied with mediocre flying, but he would have none of it.

Jou fokker' (You fucker) was his invariable opening salvo to sloppy procedures or when he found some deficiency in a pilot's knowledge. He would make the sweating pilot repeat the exercise or quiz them until they got it right. Predictably, he was soon hated throughout the squadron. But I loved him. Through his insistent nagging, I began to raise my flying skills to a much higher standard and, through constant checking, to leave my careless *loskop* ways behind me.

It was an easy decision to go with Major Fokker when it was my turn for border duty. No one else wanted to go with him.

We were sent to the air base at Grootfontein, a town in the northeast of the territory where the South African military had upgraded the airport to facilitate their operations against Swapo. Two Dakota crews were permanently based there, with one rotated every month from 25 Squadron and 44 Squadron, which was based in Pretoria. Our accommodation was comfortable, but most of our time was spent on flying intense back-to-back operations.

Our first operation began the moment we stepped off the Hercules transport plane into the searing heat of the southern African summer: an emergency casevac (casualty evacuation) from Ondangwa, a strategic military base less than 60 kilometres from the border with Angola. Luckily, Major Fokker had made me check and recheck all of the bearings on our freshly drawn war map before we'd left Cape Town.

We left our bags in the operations room and ran out to the unmarked, camouflaged C-47 with borrowed survival jackets and weapons. Ninety minutes later we were on the ground to pick up the most severely injured victims. A mine had exploded under their patrol vehicle. The men had been flown by helicopter to be sta-bilised at Ondangwa's forward hospital and await evacuation to Grootfontein.

Fokker at the Border

While the stretchers were being loaded, I wandered into the hospital tents to see what the medics were up to. I immediately wished I hadn't. The smell of burned flesh was overpowering, and I was confronted by the sight of young men around my own age lying with heaving, bloodstained chests as medics worked on their shattered bodies.

One soldier, who looked unscathed from the blast, asked a medic for a pan to urinate in. He passed a stream of blood into the container and had to be catheterised. Another's face was heavily wrapped with deeply stained bandages. He'd been looking over the side of the vehicle when the mine exploded and his face had taken the full force of the blast. The medic said his features and eyes were gone, burned off.

Towards dusk we took off with our sad load and landed at Grootfontein after dark. There we were finally able to check into the base and draw our kit, which included weapons and survival vests packed with items to help you evade capture and survive long enough to be rescued if you went down in the bush. I was disgusted to find that many vital items had been stolen from my vest. The Swiss army knife, compass and fishing gear were all missing. I damned the selfish thief to a special kind of hell.

Evacuating casualties was to become a constant and heart-breaking part of our job. Most of the injured soldiers were young conscripts doing national service before starting their adult lives. For many, their futures would be spent coping with a severe disability that would keep them permanently dependent on others. But that's war, I guess.

While many of the South African casualties were the result of landmines planted by Swapo guerrillas, perhaps even more were caused by the soldiers themselves. Access to lethal weapons, coupled with boredom and stupidity, made for a deadly combination, which often had us flying after sunset to try and save lives. Typical was a bored soldier who chose to clean his loaded weapon at night and peppered three of his sleeping friends with 7.62-mm rounds. Or the squad that lit up cigarettes after washing down the hard floor of their tent with petrol. We evacuated a dozen severely burned troops that night.

Once we also picked up a white farming family accompanying a coffin containing the remains of a relative. While most of the territory's 100 000 whites lived in towns, a smattering had remained near the Operational Area. Dozens, if not more, were killed by guerrilla landmines in the course of the Border War. In this case, the farmer had been hurt in the incident that killed his family member, but stoically climbed aboard the aircraft unaided. As there was no lower hold in the C-47, the coffin was strapped to the floor between the long bench seats. The family had to sit around it. I worried about the callousness of this until I peered into the back during the flight. They were all playing cards, using the coffin as a convenient table.

Sometimes we also evacuated wounded soldiers from Unita, South Africa's ally of convenience. I never did a casevac for a wounded enemy. It wasn't that kind of war.

We did most of our daytime flying on the border at low level or high altitude to avoid ground fire. The enemy had small arms, portable RPG-7 rocket launchers, 12.5-mm anti-aircraft guns (towed around with donkeys!) and SAM-7 heat-seeking missiles. We also varied our routes to avoid flying over the same piece of ground twice. Most of the area was ground scrub with low trees and bushes, devoid of navigational details. Global Positioning System (GPS) and other electronic navigation aids were years away from becoming widely available, so we used a map, ruler, compass and stopwatch to plot our course from one tiny airstrip to another.

Low flying at 50–100 feet for up to nine hours a day was exhausting and demanded a special technique. We trimmed the Dakota slightly nose-up, so that if you released the controls or became inattentive, it would tend to climb. That was much better than the alternative, which was flying into the ground.

We never attempted to turn at low level. We first eased up to 200 feet, banked onto our new heading and then sank down again. Sometimes we flew into drenching downpours from thunderstorms. It was not comforting to go to instrument flight (IF) with no visual references at only 100 feet, but we simply eased off the stick pressure and allowed the Dakota to climb slightly until we could see the ground again.

I'm ashamed to say we took some pleasure in scaring residents and their animals. No one ever remained upright or on their bicycles when our low-level Dakota came bearing down on them. People would drop prone on the ground, while livestock, pets and game would scatter wildly. We didn't make any friends among the locals, but as far as I know we didn't hurt anybody. We were just young guys having some rough fun.

Sometimes, we showed our nicer sides.

One of our regular C-47 missions was the 'rum run', a double visit to a number of forward bases where we would drop off personnel and cargo in the morning and pick up again later in the day. Before we were due to arrive at a forward base, troops would patrol and guard the perimeter of the airstrip to avoid mortar or other firing incidents.

Eenhana base was always our favourite. The CO would always greet our aircraft with cans of ice-cold Coca-Cola or Fanta for the crew – very welcome refreshment in the relentless heat. Once, on our second visit of the day, he looked grim. He told us that an attack on their supply convoy had left the base without enough diesel fuel, both to keep their perimeter lighting on and to pick up far-flung patrols. The troops would be forced to walk 20 kilometres back to base through enemy territory.

'Let's try to help these guys,' suggested Major Fokker after a long silence on our way back to Ondangwa, our last stop before going home. I couldn't have agreed more. We landed at Ondangwa and the major immediately telephoned the fuel depot. 'Where is our fuel, you *fokkers*,' he began. 'We have to get out of here in ten minutes.'

'What fuel, Major?'

'The nine drums of diesel for Eenhana. It should have been waiting for us on the apron. Get it here and load it on board immediately.'

'But we have no paperwork, Major.'

'That's your problem, you can look for it later. Hurry up!'

Five minutes later, a Bedford truck backed up to the Dakota. Sweating troops manhandled nine 200-litre steel drums up the sloping deck. I supervised strapping them to the floor while Major Fokker signed the Eenhana CO's name on a receipt for the unhappy-looking sergeant. We started up, took off and headed in the direction of Grootfontein as per our flight plan. Once out of sight of the airfield, we swung north towards Eenhana, arriving there just before sunset. We weren't expected but the CO met us anyway with icy drinks. 'Got something for you,' said my major, handing him the receipt. 'Go fetch your troops.'

It's amazing how much a cold drink can mean in a hot climate.

One day we were told to fly to a short gravel strip in southern Angola. A Swapo training base had been identified, bombed and then attacked by the Recces, the elite Special Forces operators. We were going there to pick up their captured booty – and what a load it was. There were bundles of Soviet-made AK-47 assault rifles bound together with string, crates of 7.62-mm ammo for the rifles, mortar rounds, a mobile 12.5-mm twin-barrel anti-aircraft gun – complete with seat and tyres – and sacks of yellow mielie meal, which our troops preferred to their own rations. They called it 'terrorist pap'.

The trouble was that the soldiers had zero concept of the weight and balance requirements of an aircraft. Their philosophy was, if it could fit into a Bedford truck, it was fine for a Dakota. We returned to our plane from a brief break to find the heavy 12.5-mm gun wedged against the rear bulkhead – a certain death trap after takeoff. It was dragged forward and tied down in a more suitable position. The troops continued to load munitions and food until the Dakota's tyres looked distinctly flat. We did our best to make it safe, but mortar rounds were still piled loosely on the floor when we took off. The soldiers weren't in the mood to leave much behind. That we made it back is a tribute to the Dakota, not good sense.

I had another encounter with the legendary Recces when Major Fokker and I were ordered to fly to Fort Doppies, the unit's operational base in the Caprivi Strip. I had no idea what to expect when we landed at their small airstrip, but I couldn't have imagined Fort Doppies anyway. Named after a local monkey that liked to put used shell casings ('doppies') into his mouth, it was immaculate, more like a rural village than an army base, with paved paths, prefab bungalows under shady trees and VIP quarters where we were to be housed for our three-day stay. And, naturally, there was great food. Luckily, we saw no sign of the lion we'd heard they tamed and allowed to wander freely around their base – Jews and lions just don't mix.

The super-friendly Recce CO explained our mission over a meal of braaied meat, yellow terrorist pap and beer. The Recces had been experimenting with dropping small 'stopper' groups to the north of a contact (firefight) to intercept and kill fleeing enemy fighters. Now the Recces wanted to see if it would be faster to parachute groups from a C-47 transport plane rather than a chopper. And they wanted to be dropped at 400 feet AGL instead of the standard 800-feet minimum. We weren't sure we'd heard correctly so we asked him to repeat the drop height. Yes, 400 feet. At that height, the chute would pop open and they'd be on the ground a moment later. There was no need for a reserve chute because by the time a jumper realised there was a problem, he'd already be dead.

The Recces piled aboard for some warm-up jumps after breakfast the next morning. We took off and looped back down the runway at 400 feet. It looked very low. The green light came on and they flung themselves out the door. A moment later, they were on the gravel strip. We circled back to land and some Recces lined up for another go. Their doctor had jumped with the first group and twisted his ankle slightly on landing. He was hobbling back for another jump when the jumpmaster turned him away at the entry door.

I was beginning to realise that these were professional soldiers who operated outside regular limits and were perhaps a little crazy on the side. Despite their friendliness towards us, I couldn't get the idea out of my head that if they received an order to liquidate the pilots, they'd instantly kill their new friends, feed us to their lion and worry about it later.

As an elite group, the Recces were allowed to choose their own weapons. They favoured the lighter, more versatile AK-47 over the more powerful South African R1. The AK-47 was also used by Swapo, which meant the Recces had an ample supply of captured AK-47s and ammunition.

I mentioned to their CO late that afternoon that I'd never fired an AK-47 before. He instantly handed me his personal weapon and sent a soldier to fetch a thousand-round case of 7.62-mm ammunition and a case of 9-mm parabellum for good measure.

The major and I retreated to their rudimentary range and fired the AK-47 and various other weapons until our ears rang. I offered to clean the rifle but the Recce officer refused. Instead, he sent us to the mess for dinner and beer. I appreciated his gesture, but I think that the real reason was that he doubted a pilot could adequately clean and service his weapon. He was probably right.

The dropping trials were not a great success. Results were erratic because it was difficult to make successive pinpoint drops at such a low level from a moving aircraft. We left Fort Doppies after agreeing that a large chopper was more suitable to deploy the small stopper groups.

Chapter 7
Pulling Rank

No sooner had I set off on my first border tour – the one with Major Fokker – than we ran into problems over that all-important military issue: rank.

We'd been at Air Force Headquarters for a full operational briefing when a red-faced captain stopped us in our tracks to growl at us: 'Don't you salute, lieutenants? Who do you think you are, strolling around like you own the place?'

Two things were responsible for this confrontation. One was that the major had a boyish face. The second was that in the Operational Area, military rank was kept hidden except for a tiny insignia on the chest. His major's castle looked little different to a lieutenant's star to a desk jockey trying to push his weight around. The major was having none of it. 'Why don't *you* salute, *jou fokker*,' he retorted and pushed his chest in the startled captain's face. He did and we walked on, leaving stuttering apologies in our wake.

The rank issue resurfaced for me when, at 20, I was promoted from co-pilot to C-47 commander. It was a controversial appointment. Aside from my age, I was still a junior lieutenant and 25 Squadron had more senior officers, including a captain who'd been my old Dakota instructor.

Major Fokker had recommended me to the squadron's new CO, who decided to make his choice after flying with all of the eligible co-pilots to assess their performances. The CO, a qualified navigator and pilot, took a long trip with each of us. He ordered us to be acting commander for the trip and to make all necessary decisions.

Because 25 Squadron did navigator training, there was a lot of specialised equipment aboard our Dakotas, including a Decca Doppler radar set with a rolling map display in the cockpit. Other navigation equipment was more basic, such as a visual drift meter for use over the ocean. It wasn't strictly necessary to use all this equipment as we flew beacon navigation using VOR (very high frequency omnidirectional radio) and ADF (automatic direction finder) on our shuttles or simply followed headings when training navigators, but as I didn't see the point of having equipment on the plane I couldn't use, I'd made it my business to learn how to use every navigation aid on the Dakota – including the temperamental Decca set.

Not every pilot took my approach, so it was a tough task when the CO asked each co-pilot during their test flight to go back to the navigator station and set up the cockpit moving-map display. This needed a good understanding of the master/slave stations that the Decca system depended on; the CO later reported to the major that I was the only one who succeeded. Some co-pilots told him it couldn't be done at all.

The CO approved my appointment to commander – to the disgust of those who felt my former instructor had been slapped in the face. Some took out their anger on me. One captain, a large Afrikaner with a short fuse, grabbed me by the lapels and, after putting his head very close to mine, hissed that the squadron pilots had a good reputation, which everyone expected me to fuck up.

He needn't have bothered. Within a few months I was grudgingly accepted as a good commander. The run-ins over rank, though, were far from over.

Although I was in charge in the cockpit, I was still only a second lieutenant on the ground. Later that year (1978), I was deployed back to the border with my good friend Neil, also a second lieutenant, as my co-pilot. The CO had agonised over sending us together because he was worried that our junior rank might make it hard for me to exercise authority. But the squadron was short of available crews and he eventually agreed to send us off – with a warning to behave.

Off we went, flying our border missions efficiently with all the confidence and gusto of youth. But as our CO had feared, my not having a castle on my chest did lead to some problems.

One night in Grootfontein the duty officer woke us up after midnight with a worried look on his face. A casevac call had just come through – and the duty C-47 crew was too drunk to fly out to pick up the casualties. There was an intense drinking culture in the SAAF; it was often said that if there'd been no drinking in World War II, there would have been no flying or fighting. But while it wasn't uncommon for air force pilots to fly only a few hours after a heavy drinking session, this was a new low: there was no tolerance for being too drunk to do your duty.

We'd been fast asleep, having just returned from a couple of days of hard flying, but we reluctantly agreed to go. We came back to find burning resentment instead of gratitude. The crew commander from 44 Squadron was a much older man at the nadir of his career. He'd disliked Neil and me on sight and often tried to pull rank on us – the mark of a poor leader. Now he'd publicly disgraced himself, and in his mind we were somehow to blame. He met our aircraft on the apron and started yelling at us the moment we stepped onto the ground. His rebuke – that we'd set him up and disrespected his rank – was ruined by the fact that he was still swaying drunk. Instead of arguing, we simply turned and walked away. The next day he returned to Pretoria for 'medical reasons' and was quickly replaced. There was no further official action taken against him; the senior officers looked after their own.

On another occasion, we were on the gravel apron at an army forward base during a rum run. A thunderstorm had just passed through and the air was hot and steamy. We'd both walked away from the aircraft to try find a cold drink and perhaps some food.

We returned to find a heap of luggage dumped in the aircraft, piled high against the rear toilet bulkhead.

'Whose luggage is this?' I asked our loadmaster, whom we had left to guard the Dakota.

'An army captain put it there,' he replied sullenly, 'and ordered me not to touch it.'

'Throw it out,' I ordered.

As I've already mentioned, the army lacked understanding of aircraft weight and balance principles. They weren't supposed to load anything aboard without crew supervision. Neil did a quick preflight check while I sat under the wing with my flying overalls stripped to the waist and ate a stale sandwich. The army captain returned to find his bags lying on the damp gravel. He turned to Neil in fury.

'Who did this, Lieutenant?' he demanded.

'I did, Captain,' he replied. 'You can't just dump your bags into an aircraft. You should know that by now.'

'Where is your commander, Lieutenant? I'm going to talk to him about your *kak* (shit) attitude.'

'There he is, Captain,' he pointed. 'He's the guy sitting under the wing without a shirt.'

As the captain marched over, I stood up and pulled on my fire-resistant Nomex overall. He saw my rank insignia and knew he was beaten. There was no point in complaining to a second lieutenant about another second lieutenant's attitude; he'd just be providing entertainment for both of us and making a fool of himself. The loadmaster supervised as the captain's muddy bags were properly loaded and then strapped to the floor. He stared at them unhappily all the way to Grootfontein.

Another time I pulled rank was far bolder.

We'd been assigned to fly to the South West African capital of Windhoek to pick up the commanding general of South African forces and his staff officers at the crack of dawn. We were to fly them to a resort camp in the Etosha National Park for a meeting with local leaders, and then to fly them back to Windhoek when they were ready.

I briefed the general and his staff before the flight, advising them – among other things – that they could not smoke on the aircraft. I'd banned smoking on all our border flights on the pretext that it distracted us during low-level flight. In reality, it was because the air circulation inside a Dakota always moves from the back of the fuselage towards the cockpit, so we could always smell what was going on in the cabin – and we both hated tobacco smoke wafting past our noses.

The staff officers, all of whom had cigarette packs bulging in their top pockets, looked at us and then at the general with disbelief, but the general finally nodded.

We were the most junior officers on the aircraft by miles.

We landed in Etosha and our smoke-deprived passengers were driven off to their meeting. We wandered off to find a swimming pool we'd spotted from the air. We swam, ate the excellent lunch that we'd asked our loadmaster to quietly set aside for us from the staff officers' hamper and lay down in the shade. We must have dozed off, because the next thing we knew, a vehicle arrived in a cloud of dust. The frantic driver gasped at us: 'The generals have been looking all over for you.' Oh shit.

He drove us at high speed to the airstrip. It was very hot and there was a knot of sweating, seriously annoyed officers standing under the wing. They actually applauded sarcastically when we arrived. We pre-flighted the C-47 in record time and I gave them another quick briefing. I got to the part about not smoking and the general held up his hand to stop me.

'Mr Schapiro,' he said, 'in view of your keeping us waiting for an hour, may we smoke on this flight?'

It wasn't a good time to stand on principle. I agreed.

I can't say that everyone obeyed my orders. One time we picked up a team of Bushmen trackers and an army officer from a forward base. After a month in the bush they smelled so bad we literally gagged in the hot cockpit until we got into the air. The officer had translated our instructions to the trackers not to use the small 'bathroom' – a seat over a small bucket that, disgustingly, had to be emptied after each use – at the back of the Dakota.

I was already familiar with unpleasant in-flight toilet experiences. When I left Ysterplaat for my first border tour, Major Fokker and I had boarded a C-160 Transall transport aircraft for our first stop in Pretoria. The plane was chock-full of soldiers and other personnel heading for the Operational Area. We sat in four long rows on canvas seats under dim fluorescent lights. There were no windows or bathrooms.

The major and I had enjoyed a delicious curry lunch before we boarded. Halfway into the three-hour flight, my stomach started to complain about the spicy food. The major was fast asleep next to me. I told myself I could wait until Pretoria. Then a severe cramp assured me I couldn't.

I crabbed forward between outsprawled legs towards the loadmaster, who radioed my predicament to the cockpit. I was sweating freely by then. Two crewmen waded through the troops to the back of the aircraft and began moving luggage away from an area near the rear ramp.

Eventually they uncovered a folding steel toilet, which they erected with a flourish. A curtain was produced and slung around the crude contraption. They then beckoned readiness. The ruckus had woken up most of the soldiers, who now craned their necks to see which lucky person was being summoned.

I was beyond modesty. I tore towards the curtained loo and flung myself onto the seat, amid loud laughter. But the joke was on them. This was not a flushable toilet. There was also no toilet paper in the cubicle, so I poked my head out to request some from the loadmaster. He muttered into his headset mike and a few moments later, a toilet roll was handed out from the cockpit to the closest passenger. He passed it to his neighbour, who passed it to the next, and so on until it was handed to me in the back cubicle.

By now, every single passenger was involved in my toilet experience except Major Fokker, who slept through it all. He wakened only when I returned to my seat, whereupon he sniffed and informed me that the plane stank like shit.

Now I watched our reeking Bushmen passengers deplane after being told not to use the bucket. One tracker had such a smirk on his face that Neil said, 'He's done something.' Indeed he had. The tracker had deposited what looked like a week's worth of poop in the bucket – including the single longest stool I'd ever seen.

We didn't enjoy our boerewors dinner that evening.

Chapter 8
Bad Behaviour on the Border

The phone rang in Grootfontein's flight operations office and we got the type of call young pilots dream about: 'Could three officers please come to a dance on Saturday night at a teachers' college?' We could! The only group we loved more than teachers were nursing students, who tended to be even wilder. Neil and I were officers, of course, but our loadmaster wasn't. We solved the problem by borrowing someone's shoulder tabs with two lieutenant stars for him to wear – technically allowing him to outrank us.

The college was in a small town about two hours' drive from Grootfontein. We danced traditional *sokkie-sokkie* numbers and drank beer until the college chaperones unkindly pushed us out the door in the early hours of the morning. Not a nice way to treat invited guests, even rowdy drunk ones. We drove through the small town and loaded a few interesting road signs onto our vehicle to use as room decorations. We had our weapons with us – me an Uzi submachine gun, Neil a 9-mm pistol and our loadmaster an R1 rifle – because Swapo had made some deep infiltrations in recent months. A few months later, a family would be ambushed and killed on the same road, but fortunately we had no problems on the long drive back.

Still, the constant awareness of danger didn't stop us, and may even have precipitated our getting into other mischief when we could.

One time, we landed at Windhoek's Eros airport on a routine mission and noticed another SAAF Dakota parked on the apron.

Unlike our camouflage C-47, it was a silver VIP machine from 44 Squadron. The cowls had been removed from one engine and we could see the legs of a mechanic perched on a work stand beneath it. We wandered over and to find out who the VIPs were.

They turned out to be a group of 20 foreign journalists on a three-day viewing/propaganda tour of the border area. Unfortunately, their plane had broken down on its first stop and needed some replacement parts flown up from Pretoria. We were about to leave the airport for our hotel when we got an urgent message. Our mission was cancelled and we were to fly the journalists to Rundu, where we'd receive further orders. But first we were to sweep out and clean the inside of our Dakota. We were also told to look after the journalists carefully and try not to cause an international incident.

Our loadmaster did his cleaning best (which was not much), but our oil-stained machine was bare bones and stripped down for utility, not comfort. We signalled that we were ready for passengers and were amused at the incongruous sight of white-jacketed stewards loading boxes of VIP food and liquor onto our camouflaged Dakota. Then the group of journalists climbed tentatively on board, looked about nervously and strapped themselves to the unpadded bench seats.

I lightheartedly assured them they were in much better hands than before. In addition, as they were now in a camouflaged 'War Dak', they'd get a taste of real border flying. We took off and circled over Eros to gain altitude. Then we set the heading to Rundu for the high-altitude sector. After a while, I popped back to see how everyone was doing. The journalists were fascinated at how young Neil and I were and started to ask questions. They'd arrived with fixed ideas about white South Africans, but soon realised we had little love for the apartheid government and weren't the Nazi stereotypes they were expecting to see. By the time we landed at Rundu, we were all getting along swimmingly. It helped that some of the women were very attractive.

At Rundu the CO and his senior staff met the aircraft and whisked the journalists away for a briefing. After the lecture, they were allowed to speak to army troops who'd been assembled on the parade ground for that purpose. This caused more than a frisson of excitement among the women-starved young troops. Some of the European female journalists were wearing loose-fitting tops that revealed more than they realised, especially when they bent down. The soldiers began to jostle each other to get closer to them. Clearly, the staff hadn't thought this one through.

After the ill-considered meeting with the troops, the Rundu staff cemented their obtuseness by taking the journalists into the bush, where an armoured vehicle with a mounted 0.50 Browning machine gun was waiting for them. A gunner demonstrated the weapon by blasting a dozen trees to splinters before the shocked journalists were then invited to have a go for themselves. The international press corps clearly didn't share the military view that destroying trees was a good time, so I jumped onto the vehicle myself and let rip. It wasn't every day that the army laid on a heavy weapon for our entertainment.

We flew the journalists to Ondangwa the next morning, where they were to be met by the repaired VIP Dakota for the rest of the border tour. The officers' mess was preparing a special braai for the journalists so we decided to make our own campfire nearby. Senior officers weren't our idea of good company, not that we were invited to the braai anyway.

Shortly after we got our fire going, one of the reporters came over to say hi. Actually, she came over to flirt. Others began wandering over from the formal braai, to the annoyance of the CO. He strode over to our noisy group and pulled us aside. 'You guys are dominating the conversation,' he warned. 'I want you to stop it.' Full of beer bravery, Neil replied, 'Commandant, we weren't invited to your braai and it looks like they don't want to be there either.'

The next morning, we received a stern lecture from the CO,

followed by a warning. He was thinking of punishing us by sending us home. This made little sense, as being sent home from the border was hardly punishment. Being sent *to* the border was punishment. Perhaps he was so upset that he forgot where he was. Our foreign charges arrived and climbed enthusiastically into our War Dak without a trace of nervousness. We set off for Ondangwa at low level, which thrilled our new best friends. The silver VIP Dakota was parked on the Ondangwa apron, and we reluctantly handed our charges back to the system.

We'd told our loadmaster to try to put some VIP liquor aside for us on the flight. As usual, he went too far and stole an entire box of Scotch miniatures that they could not fail to miss. In self-defence, we went on the attack and reported, on our return to Grootfontein operations, that the stewards had left half a box of liquor on the plane. What should we do with it?

The problem, and half of the liquor, went away.

Another time, I returned from a long flight to hear a familiar voice in the Grootfontein ATC tower. It was my 'twin', Kasteen. We'd met at the SAAF College when she was a qualified military air traffic controller, a big-boned blonde of German heritage who was born on the same day and in the same year as me. We were shockingly similar, except that she outranked me.

Kasteen and I would cross paths many times in the next few years. We always liked each other but never became romantically involved. Now she'd arrived for a tour of duty on the border. We met at the officers' club that evening and caught up. She still outranked me and was also learning to fly. She was taking a private pilot's course in Pretoria and asked if I'd fly a few circuits and landings with her. Of course, I agreed.

When South African forces invaded southern Angola, they had overrun a few small airfields. Retreating Angolan forces had abandoned some unserviceable light aircraft that had probably belonged to private Portuguese owners during the colonial era. They'd been repaired and were now in SAAF service at Grootfontein. One of them was a small single-engine Piper that was suitable for flying training, and it was this aircraft that Kasteen wanted to fly. Unfortunately, the plane needed some work, and by the time it was pronounced fully serviceable, Kasteen had tower duty.

It seemed a pity to waste such fine flying weather. There was no other traffic at the airport apart from a Safair Hercules that had been parked there all day, so I offered to man the tower while she did a couple of circuits with Neil.

I knew very little about air traffic control except for what I heard at the other end of the radio, but Kasteen agreed because it was so quiet and she'd be on tower frequency in the Piper anyway. The little Piper started up and I gave them taxi and takeoff clearance.

I was enjoying watching a takeoff from this unusual vantage point when, to my surprise, someone radioed the tower. A chopper was starting up and requested clearance to Ondangwa. I advised him about the Piper and cleared him to lift off and to keep the traffic in sight on his departure. To my shock, another call followed. A SAAF light aircraft was inbound at low level and wanted to join the circuit. I ordered him to climb to circuit height and gave him our current weather, more or less, and the runway in use.

May he do a straight-in approach instead, he inquired.

'No,' yelled Kasteen from the Piper.

'No,' I confirmed, 'use the active runway.'

This pretend ATC stuff was becoming a bit too real.

Now the Safair Hercules got into the action and called for start clearance for Windhoek. I was getting into the swing of things and gave them weather data from the tower instruments, along with the runway in use. The big Hercules taxied out and I gave them a complicated departure clearance that I largely made up. I told them to keep the Piper in sight and cleared them for takeoff.

By then Kasteen had had enough of the growing farce. The Piper did a full stop landing, taxied in and shut down.

She rushed upstairs, claiming to be very pleased with my performance, and quickly sent telexes to Ondangwa and Windhoek about their incoming traffic, something I didn't know I had to do.

We'd got away with it. But we didn't try that ATC switcheroo again.

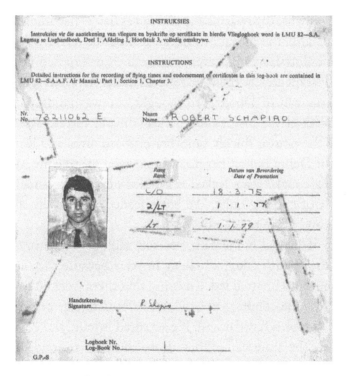

The first page of my SAAF logbook

Then there was our farm adventure. A friendly Afrikaans farmer in the Grootfontein area invited us over for an evening braai. We arrived to find him and his wife standing under a beautiful pepper tree. His wife was holding a bloody ripsaw.

They had slaughtered a cow earlier in the afternoon and she'd just finished sawing the legs off the carcass. We were extra-polite to her, as befitted someone holding a gore-spattered saw, helping them hoist the bloody haunches and other meaty cuts up into the pepper tree to tenderise them overnight.

As the sun set behind the pepper tree with its dangling, fleshy fruit, we sat outside on the concrete stoep. They weren't a chatty couple, and were given to long silences between sentences. The wife, heavy, prim and reserved, wore a billowing yellow frock that exposed only her lower arms and the calves below her ample knees. As it got dark, the mosquitos began to bite like crazy. We rolled down our shirtsleeves but every square inch of exposed flesh was under constant attack. Then she reached under her chair and pulled out a spray can of Doom. We thought she was going to give a few spritzes of the insecticide to clear the air. Instead she began to spray the poison thickly onto her exposed arms and legs until rivulets of Doom ran off her flesh. I managed to stifle my laughter down to a cough. Tears leaked from Neil's eyes as he shook with the effort of keeping quiet. We both needed quite a few shots of Klippies and Coke to calm down.

Over delicious homemade venison sausage, the farmer told us that they hadn't taken a holiday in years because they couldn't leave their dogs unattended. Knowing that there were no missions planned for the coming weekend, we offered to stay on the farm while they took a few days off. He accepted instantly.

When the time came, they drove away in a cloud of dust, leaving us a refrigerator full of raw meat and a table full of warm liquor. Just like that, we had our own farm for the weekend. We took a drive to look around, thinking we could perhaps use our Uzis to take an opportunistic shot at something edible. Being un-trained and noisy, we saw little apart from some wild guinea fowl so we gave up and returned to the easier option of the farmer's refrigerator and brandy.

But the best part of the evening was the rockets.

Bad Behaviour on the Border

We'd discovered that fireworks were freely available in Windhoek and had made an impulse buy of six huge exploding rockets and a dozen jumping jacks. We'd already put the jumpers to good use in the army officers' bar but still had all our rockets.

The farmer had told us that next to his farm was a tightly guarded army transit camp for troops headed to the forward areas. They'd been warned by military police that deserters from the camp could be dangerous and should be shot on sight if they approached the house. After finishing our braai, we carefully tilted a rocket and sent it whooshing in the direction of the camp. It exploded overhead in a thunderous shower of green and red sparks. Shortly afterwards, we heard yelling and screamed orders.

We sent one over each night we were there.

PART 2

THE SAA YEARS

Chapter 9
The Royal Family

It was 1979. I'd finally made it to South African Airways. And there I was, a lowly in-flight relief 'boy pilot' on my first airline flight – watching my captain pass out drunk on the floor of a public train in Lisbon.

I noted through my own alcoholic fog that he was lying out on his back in the middle of the aisle, clutching his bottle of home-made wine as it gurgled its contents onto the floor. A human island. Whenever the train stopped or started, a river of red flowed around him, pooling at the end of the carriage until the tide sent it in the opposite direction.

When I joined SAA it was ruled over by two distinct groups: Afrikaner political appointees and the Royal Family.

On the ground, all senior SAA executives were Broeder-bonders, members of the secretive Afrikaner 'brotherhood' that dominated South Africa's governing National Party and state-owned entities such as the airline and railways. The children of political appointees were more easily accepted into the airline as pilots. Mistrusted and disliked by the regular pilots, they acquired derogatory nicknames, such as *'Pa sê'* (Father says). Only Broederbond members could expect to be appointed to top positions; better-qualified English-speakers had to be content with middle management posts.

In the air, though, the Royal Family reigned supreme. They were mostly former World War II pilots, and they ran SAA flight operations with an iron hand. Notoriously indifferent to the opinions of their crews, these captains expected the other pilots to follow orders without question – even if those instructions contradicted the official procedures in the Boeing manual.

The drunken captain on the train in Lisbon was a member of the Royal Family.

The drinking had begun as soon as we landed in the Portuguese capital. During our descent, the cabin crew chief brought each of us a paper bag with beer 'for the bus'. I learned that this was an airline tradition, with the amount of alcohol in the bag depending on the length of the ride to the hotel. Mauritius was a three-beer trip; London and Frankfurt were two. Our trip to the Lisbon Sheraton was just one.

In those days, we checked into hotels according to a strict pecking order. Cockpit and cabin crew (about 19 on a 747) typically did not stay in the same hotels on layovers, as our pilots' union had ensured that we usually got better accommodation than cabin staff – one of their many sources of resentment against us. (They also felt it was unfair that we got more concession tickets for our families. Aside from an allocated number of free tickets every year, my wife got an 'orange pass' that she could use to book a standby ticket at a 90 per cent discount off the full fare.)

However, we did stay in the same place in destinations where there was only one suitable hotel. Until the ritual broke down in later years and it became a free-for-all at the desk, the captain always checked in first, followed by the rest of the cockpit crew and finally the cabin staff.

After checking in, we collected our meal allowance from the cashier, a daily amount paid out in local currency for subsistence on the trip. The amount they gave us was calculated according to the cost of eating three meals a day in our respective hotels, which enabled us to eat well at local cafés and restaurants that were invariably cheaper than our hotels. One exception was New York, where local restaurant prices often exceeded the menu prices at our seedy

The Royal Family

Sightseeing in Portugal

Leaving for a flight from my London hotel

midtown hotel. In the Big Apple, we often ran out of meal allowance even if we ate mostly in bars, cheap joints and at deli counters. I remember making a couple of 'midnight runs' from floor to floor collecting uneaten bread rolls, butter and jam to eat the next day.

In places like Lisbon, though, we were always flush with local money, which we called 'Monopoly money', and could rarely use it all despite spending freely on food, drink and local travel. (Within a few years, it would be the South African rand that became 'Monopoly money'.)

The Lisbon captain ordered us to meet for a drink in the co-pilot's room in stripped-down uniform – another long-standing tradition. I dumped my bags, removed my jacket, tie and shoulder tabs and found my way to the co-pilot's room. The captain and the flight engineer were already there. We each put money into a pot and I was sent out to buy beer. Luckily, the tradition had changed a little: I was told that in the old days, boy pilots like me were expected to buy post-flight beer out of their own meal allowance. The beer party lasted two hours – short by airline standards – and we set a meeting time for dinner before all tottering off to bed.

The captain chose where he wanted us all to eat – and what he wanted that night was a restaurant that specialised in roasted quail. It was a subway and train ride away, but I didn't mind the distance because everything was new and exciting. We were joined by a few senior air hostesses and I wondered why more of the cabin crew didn't want to come with us for dinner. I soon found out.

After a few stops to have drinks on the short walk from the train station, we arrived at the restaurant. The captain ordered quail for everyone, irrespective of whether they wanted it or not. The quails were served on long skewers, like kebabs. I had some qualms about eating such tiny birds but must admit they were delicious. Our table ordered bottle after bottle of local red wine. The empties weren't removed from the table but piled to one side. This was a common practice in Lisbon eateries, which later totted up the empty bottles, but the quail place offered an unusual twist. They refilled the empties with their homemade wine, real rotgut stuff, as a thank-you gift.

We divided the moderate food bill and ridiculous liquor bill between us (now I knew why cabin crew hated eating out with pilots) and staggered drunkenly to the station with our refilled gifts in hand. The flight engineer lay down on the track and put his ear on one of the rusty rails. He said he could hear a train coming but couldn't see it yet. This was not surprising, because it was coming from the other direction. We hauled him off the track.

We climbed up the metal steps into the almost empty carriage and dropped gratefully onto the wooden seats. The captain began to slump in his seat, gradually sliding onto the floor. We left him there until we reached our stop.

It had been risky for me to move from the SAAF to SAA. While most SAA pilots did come from the air force, there were strict rules governing how and when a SAAF pilot could apply to the national carrier. The idea was to avoid our using the air force merely as a stepping stone to the airline – which of course it was.

Pilots were not allowed to appear before an SAA selection committee unless they'd already resigned from the SAAF. The problem, of course, was that if you didn't get into SAA, you'd be without any job at all. I decided to mitigate the risk by making sure I was as well-qualified as possible before I applied to the airline.

I'd started preparing when I returned to normal squadron life in Cape Town after my last border stint. After four years in the air force, and with sufficient flight hours under my belt, I decided I needed to get my senior commercial licence as soon as possible.

It was unusual to pass all of the tough senior commercial exams on the first attempt, but I was determined to try. I attended classes from 7 to 10 pm three times a week in a classroom at the

University of Cape Town, which was the closest I ever came to attending university. There were seven required subjects, the easiest being meteorology. I worked hard at the other six and briefly studied the easier met material. As a result, I passed everything except meteorology.

SAA held one of its infrequent pilot recruiting drives shortly after I passed meteorology on my second try. I sent my letter of resignation to the SAAF at the same time as I sent my application to SAA. The airline sent me a flight voucher to travel to Johannesburg for medical exams at their small clinic in the SAA building at Jan Smuts airport, as OR Tambo International was then called. There was the usual battery of physical, aptitude and psychological tests. Successful applicants were invited back to Johannesburg for a flight test in a Hawker Siddeley twin-turboprop aircraft, the smallest aircraft in the SAA fleet, and a final interview.

Eight of us had nervously boarded the Hawker for our evening flight test. The co-pilot was a real dick who kept grinning at us and laughing like a hyena, which made us feel worse. We were impressed that SAA had loaded two meals for each of us in the galley oven and made the mistake of gobbling them down. The greasy airline food rapidly turned to lead in our bellies as we took turns at pulling and pushing to maintain altitude during steep turns. As a C-47 pilot, I was used to heavy flight controls, so I had no major problems with the flight check other than the co-pilot and the nausea.

The final interview was before a panel of senior airline pilots and executives. They already knew that, as a SAAF pilot, I could fly well. The question was whether I could fit into an airline environment. New pilots in SAA always started as in-flight relief pilots irrespective of the position they had held before, but the panel was looking to hire future SAA captains, not relief pilots. My early promotion to C-47 commander, and the fact that I'd already passed the senior commercial exams, convinced them that I was suitable.

I was accepted into SAA at the age of 21, the minimum age one can legally hold a senior commercial licence.

Shortly after I got in, SAA terminated all pilot recruitment for six long years. Luckily, and unknown to me, my mentor Major Fokker (no longer a major) had been accepted a few months earlier.

As third pilots on Boeing 747 international operations, we were known as boy pilots. Our job involved much of the preparation and grunge work in the cockpit, such as inputting waypoints into the navigation system, filling in the flight log, folding waste bags and bringing hot towels to the primary crew. Our main job was ATC communication and in-flight relief to enable the primary crew to get a few hours' rest before landing.

My former major, who'd already completed his initial course and was starting to do overseas trips, helped me arrange to rent a room in the same house he was boarding at near the airport. He also advised me to take the conversion course to the new aircraft very seriously.

Our lectures covered Boeing 747 technical information, international air law, emergency equipment, inertial navigation, Jeppesen route manuals, 747 flight manuals (volumes 1–3) and 747 performance. The final phase was simulator training, followed by a check. It all seemed impossibly exciting to me. All through the course, I kept imagining that some official would walk into the classroom and say, 'Sorry guys, there's been a mistake and we don't need any more pilots, you can all go home now.'

We ate each day in the SAA cafeteria we called 'The Greasy Spoon'. It may have been the only restaurant in the world that actually closed for 45 minutes over lunch time so that the staff could eat their own meals.

During one too-early lunch, I heard my name being called. I looked around and, to my surprise and the amazement of my classmates, saw a beautiful air hostess smiling and waving at me. Seeing my obvious confusion, she told me she'd been two years behind me at Herzlia. She was the person who told me that Herzlia teachers had started citing my flying story as an example of perseverance. The cheek was unbelievable, but it was nice to be noticed, especially by her.

My early days in the airline quickly made it clear to me that SAA had a toxic drinking culture every bit as bad as the SAAF. Many older captains were functioning alcoholics, protected by their crews' silence and an old-boy system from any consequences for their excesses and with zero pressure from the airline to change.

They also treated us as if they were feudal lords and we their serfs. On one crew bus ride to the hotel, the captain invited all of the air hostesses to dinner with him that evening. It was an offer they couldn't refuse, so later we all sat around a large table at a restaurant of his choice. When the bill arrived, he grabbed it and loudly announced he was paying for everyone. The young flight attendants were hugely impressed, which was probably the object of the exercise. In truth, I was a little impressed myself – until the next morning, when I found a handwritten note pushed under my door informing me of my portion of the previous night's bill. The captain had simply divided the full amount between the pilots and expected us to repay him for the meals eaten by the women he'd invited.

I paid, of course. This was the same captain who'd achieved airline notoriety by trying to smuggle rhino horn out of South Africa. He'd stashed it in a small suitcase that he asked another pilot to take overseas. Unluckily for the captain, customs officials found the horn during one of their periodic searches of aircrew bags. Trading in rhino horn had been banned by CITES, the international convention governing the global wildlife trade, since 1977. Anyone else would have gone to jail. Captain Rhino Horn's political connections allowed him to escape without serious consequences. You don't piss off someone with those kinds of friends. (To add insult to injury, I was later told that Rhino Horn had a management dining expense account for his meals. Not only was he currying favour with the air hostesses, he was making a nice profit off his cockpit crew as well.) I didn't eat out with him again.

I soon got used to other outrageous behaviour on overseas trips. In a few short months, nothing would seem outrageous any more. And I quickly learned that it wasn't wild drunken partying that got you into trouble; it was refusing to participate in it.

When I got back to Johannesburg after that first five-day trip to Lisbon, I realised that neither I nor my liver wanted to live like this. I could party as hard as anyone, but now I was being forced to drink whether I wanted to or not, something I'd always hated in the SAAF.

I made a decision to have one drink for every two or three of the going rate. Yes, our bill-sharing system meant I'd be paying for other pilots' drinks, but I'd have to accept that. I resolved to join the captain and crew for some drinks and dinners, especially on the first night, but I also wanted to explore foreign cities and take day trips into the countryside, not just see the inside of the nearest bars. I knew there'd be a cost to this non-conformist behaviour, but as I was already regarded as an oddity for being Jewish – something still remarked upon almost daily – I thought I could get away with it. I did.

Later, I spoke quietly to my mentor, the former major, about my concerns, carefully trying not to seem critical of anyone in particular. My conversation revealed something that I'd find to be a constant truth throughout my flying career: if something is worrying you, it's probably also worrying a lot of other people as well.

It turned out that a lot of the newer pilots were deeply unhappy with the status quo. We were a different generation of flyers who were healthier, watched our weight, exercised regularly and smoked and drank much less than older aviators who lived by the work hard, play hard credo. Many of us had little interest in being drawn into the self-destructive behaviour of the Royal Family,

Maand/Jaar Month/Year SEP/OCT 1979		Gesagvoerder Captain	Leerling, mede-vliegnier of tweede vlieënier / Pupil, co-pilot or second pilot	Taak (Insluitende resultate en opmerkings) Task (Including results and remarks)	Vliegtuig Aircraft	
Dag Day	Uur Hour				Tipe Type	No./ Letter
					(Totale o/b) (Totals b/f)	
SEP 1	2020	BARKER	SELF	LON-CPT	747SP	ZS-SPE
11	1540	LANGE	SELF	JS-WHK-LIS	747SP	ZS-SPB
13	0730	LANGE	SELF	LIS-ROM-ATH-ROM-LIS	747SB	ZS-SAM
17	2155	LANGE	SELF	LIS-JS	747SP	ZS-SP
26	0620	TAINTON	SELF	JS-DN-MRU-PER-SYD	747SB	ZS-SAN
OCT 2	0200	TAINTON	SELF	SYD-PER-MRU-DN-JS	747SB	ZS-SAM
9	1610	BARKER	SELF	JS-SID-LHR	747SB	ZS-SAL
13	1950	BARKER	SELF	LHR-CPT	747SP	ZS-SPB
19	1650	HUGO	SELF	WHK-SID-DUSSEL-FRA	747SB	ZS-SAM
21	1115	HUGO	SELF	FRA-AMS-FRA	747SP	ZS-SPO
24	1640	HUGO	SELF	FRA-LPA-WHK	747SB	ZS-SAP
29	0745	ROSSOUW	SELF	JS-MRU	747SB	ZS-SAO
30	1800	ROSSOUW	SELF	MRU-JS	747SB	ZS-SAO
		SUMMARY :	FOR SEPT/OCT 1979		BOEING 747	
		DATE :	2-11-79		BOEING 747 TOTAL	
		SIGNATURE				
Groottotaal Grand total 270		Ure Hrs. 45	Min. Mins.	(Totale o/d) (Totals c/f ....)		

A page from my SAA logbook shows flights to destinations such as London, Lisbon and Frankfurt.

and others were also trying make a partial withdrawal without offending or criticising anyone.

Within a few years, the pilots' union started to quietly put pressure on the heaviest drinkers to accept help. Around the same time, international airlines adopted a type of training called Crew Resource Management (CRM). This was developed after the biggest disaster in aviation history, the 1977 runway collision between two 747s that killed 583 people on the Spanish island of Tenerife. Miscommunication and a reluctance by pilots to question a captain's decision had led a highly trained KLM crew to believe they had clearance to commence takeoff when a Pan Am plane was still crossing the runway.

CRM taught crews to operate as captain-led teams in which all members contribute information and are encouraged to speak up if they see a problem or are unhappy about something in the cockpit. It was the polar opposite of the 'Do what I tell you and speak when you're spoken to' attitude of the Royal Family captains, which meant you only had one person thinking in the cockpit instead of three. Some older captains refused to do CRM at all. Others failed the course or simply walked out. As CRM was now a legal requirement to fly, they effectively retired themselves.

With the demise of the Royal Family, an individual captain's opinion lost its power to have devastating consequences on your career. The cast-iron 'socialising' rules that forced a cockpit crew to eat, drink and hang out together on trips cracked wide open and everyone became free to do their own thing when overseas. Only once the Royal Family were gone did a new air of professionalism settle over SAA.

Political appointees never quite disappeared. They just changed masters and continued to plague SAA.

Chapter 10
Battling the Bulge

It wasn't unusual for boy pilots and cabin staff to gain ten kilograms or more in their first year of working for SAA.

A fact that may come as a shock to today's abused traveller is that airline food used to be surprisingly good – even in economy class.

First-class food, though, was in a league of its own. Canapés, appetisers such as caviar and foie gras, soups, main courses such as lobster and fillet steak, lavish desserts and rich cheese and fruit trays were of fine restaurant quality. Meats such as rare roast beef, game or duck would be carved to order on board; nothing was pre-packed.

We had crew meals provided for us, but I was advised by another pilot on my very first flight that I should wait until the passengers in first had eaten. Boy, was he right. There was no such thing as 'limited choice' in first class, so ample supplies of every dish were loaded – and it was all available to the pilots once the passengers had been served. (Sometimes even before, if the truth be known.)

Economic realities gradually forced all airlines to cut back on costly food items until airline food mostly became the ghastly paste it is today. Even crew meals were downgraded to economy-style food in foil containers. But back then our problem was stopping eating, especially as we knew all uneaten food would be thrown out at our destination. Crew members packed on weight until they learned to stop using their bodies as waste bins for leftover food, however tasty.

Battling the Bulge

But that wasn't our only battle of the bulge during those years.

Our flights to Europe took hours longer than any other international carrier. This was because many African governments denied overflight rights to SAA in protest against apartheid, forcing us to fly out over the Atlantic Ocean and around the protruding 'bulge' of West Africa. In the 15 years I was with SAA, the intensifying sanctions campaign against Pretoria meant that we also lost landing rights at important destinations in the United States and Australia.

We did, however, keep our landing rights at Ilha do Sal, a small island in the Cape Verde group off the west coast of Africa. Most SAA flights to Europe and America stopped there for refuelling and a crew change, forcing us to spend so much time there that we called it our home away from home. Actually, it was more like an isolated beach shack than a home – and we liked to say that your best day in Sal was the day you left.

The island was barren, with little besides a small fishing industry, some sea-salt pans and the modern airport, which SAA's money helped to maintain. The airport was then Cape Verde's biggest single source of income, with 36 flights stopping there every week in the early 1980s. (A *New York Times* report from that period says that the weekly number dropped to nine European-bound planes after Washington banned SAA flights from the US, costing the former Portuguese colony more than US$7 million a year.)

For the first few years, only cockpit crew broke their journeys in Sal; cabin staff would continue non-stop to the destination. We'd be pretty tired by the time we got there. There was no air traffic control for much of the bulge route; airlines that regularly flew in African airspace had developed a system of position reporting independent of the continent's notoriously poor ATC system. At most waypoints round the bulge we'd relay our position report on two different frequencies to ensure safe vertical separation. We also monitored a third emergency channel. It kept us quite busy.

On arrival, though, there was little to do in those days but eat, drink beer, play table tennis and stroll along the endless beach. (Trust me, it gets boring quickly.) As flight and duty rules tightened, flight attendants insisted that they also do a crew change in Sal. I think they soon realised they'd had the better deal before, but by then it was too late to change their minds.

Some pilots got permission from the local government to keep a twin-engine speedboat at the hotel, which they used to catch game fish that they filleted, froze and took back to South Africa. *Springbok 1*, as the boat was named, was later sold to island residents and replaced by the larger *Springbok 2*.

Ironically, we occasionally got a chance for some impromptu political détente. Sal was also a convenient stopover for Cubana, the Cuban national airline, on its flights between the Soviet Union and Havana. Cuba and South Africa fought on opposite sides in Angola, but SAA and Cubana aircraft were forced into an uneasy truce when they shared the Sal airport apron.

By that stage my SAAF career was over. I'd had to buy out my remaining Permanent Force service when I joined SAA and I never flew a SAAF aircraft again. The military wasn't yet done with me, though: I was still required to serve six years in the Citizen Force.

In the early 1980s, I was called up once to serve a month-long tour as an operations officer at Ondangwa. My enduring memory of that month was going to bed in my tent on the first night. To protect the large base from attack, the most vulnerable areas were floodlit throughout the night. The rest were considered 'speculative sectors' where heavy mortars were fired at random to discourage night attacks.

No one bothered to tell me this interesting fact. Or that my tent was close to a speculative sector.

I was just dropping off to sleep when an enormous explosion lifted me out of my bunk. It was followed by another and yet another, creeping ever closer to my tent. My adrenaline and heart were pumping away and I was about to roll onto the floor when I noticed my tent mate hadn't even stirred. 'You'll get used to it,' he muttered and went back to sleep.

He was right. By the end of the tour, the 120-mm mortar blasts went almost unnoticed.

Now, on Sal, we were getting a chance to meet people allied to those we'd been firing the mortars at.

Sometimes the Cubana crews, complete with a political commissar and a few burly air hostesses, also stayed at our stone-walled hotel. They mostly kept strictly to themselves, but a few times, lured by curiosity and away from the watchful eye of their commissar, they'd join us on the beach for a few drinks.

Aside from these interludes, there wasn't much else to do or see on Sal. About twice a year, a small merchant ship would anchor offshore to load up with 50-kg bags of sea salt from the pans. Sometimes the heavy sacks fell into the sea while being lowered onto a skiff from the wooden jetty and then rowed out to the rust-stained ship. No one seemed to care.

Another thing the Verdeans didn't seem to care about was the numerous sharks that would circle the island; we'd watch screaming kids trying to leap onto the creatures as they cruised past the jetty. Against my better judgement, I once spent a few hours fishing on *Springbok 1*. Two of every three game fish the guys hooked that morning were lost to the ferocious sharks before they could be reeled in. Endlessly patient, the black fins kept circling our little boat, waiting for more hooked fish or someone to fall in. I never went again.

Years later, I would again try my hand at fishing, this time in Alaska, where in summertime the rivers and streams teem with salmon swimming upstream to spawn. Each type of salmon has its own short season, with king salmon being the most desirable catch. I bought a suitable rod and tackle at the local military surplus store and paid the exorbitant non-resident permit fee.

Serious fishermen travel for hours to get to their best fishing spots, where they keep a wary eye open for bears, who also know the best spots to feed on the swarming salmon to fatten up for winter. At the bottom of the desirability scale is Ship Creek, a river that runs right through the centre of Anchorage. Due to its easy accessibility, every bum, layabout or drunk goes there to try to hook a fish for dinner. They stand elbow to elbow, jostling and cursing each other in a rough sport called 'combat fishing'. Serious fishermen would not be seen dead at Ship Creek, but as we were in Anchorage for less than 24 hours, I decided to give combat fishing a go.

It was early and most drunks were still sleeping it off. I found a gap between two burly locals, one wearing waders and standing slightly into the stream. They seemed to know what they were doing, so I observed them for a few moments. The trick seemed to be to cast slightly upstream and allow your lure to be pulled by the current while slowly hauling it in. I tried to do the same with my new rod, but it was a lousy cast, and within moments my line was far downstream. I started to reel it in when I felt some resistance on the line. A bite!

I jerked the rod hard and the wading guy next to me nearly toppled over. He lifted his leg and I could see my red lure stuck firmly into his rubber boot. I must say he was decent about it, perhaps because he didn't want to ruin his waders. He patiently worked the hook out and handed it back to me without a word.

Determined to do better, I cast again. It was a decent distance but yet again, the lure moved rapidly downstream. I felt erratic movement on the line and jerked hard. The wader's rod was nearly ripped from his hands. I had indeed hooked a big one. This time he wasn't so nice. He pulled out a huge Bowie knife and cut my line to pieces while looking at me to see what I was going to do about it. 'Thank you, sir,' I said and moved away from angry wader and his glaring friend before they decided to use me for salmon bait.

I moved upstream along the bank until I found a dam that the porter at our hotel had mentioned. The crowd was much thinner there, so I tied on another lure and gave a huge cast, my best yet.

Shopping for souvenirs in Alaska with my father-in-law, Les Getz

Unfortunately, I had not noticed a steel cable stretched from bank to bank in front of the dam wall. My expensive lure flew over the cable and within moments the line had spun itself tightly around the wire. I gaped at my latest fuck-up and gave the line a couple of experimental tugs. It was clearly attached for life. I cut my own line and morosely tied on my final lure.

I was about to try again when my captain arrived and asked how the fishing was going. 'Okay,' I lied. Then he noticed the lure dangling off the cable. 'Look at that,' he exclaimed, laughing, 'some dumb bastard has got his lure stuck on the cable.'

'Where?' I asked and laughed along with him. He left and after a few minutes I followed, leaving the rod on the bank.

My combat fishing experience proved – yet again – that I was an unlucky fisherman. And who knows what the sharks would have done to me if I'd got back onto *Springbok 1*.

Lunch was the main event of the day on Ilha do Sal. The food wasn't good and had to be rescued with the aid of a range of stinging hot sauces. Still, everyone stayed at the table, drawing out the meal for hours. By late afternoon most of us had gone to bed to get some rest before the post-midnight call for our next flight.

Call time came in the form of 'Shorty', a small, grizzled local with a grubby SAA cap on his head. He'd hammer on each door in turn and yell 'Calling time' until he got a response. Then came a shock for those not wise in the ways of Sal: there was often no water in the rooms in the early morning hours. Not just no *hot* water, no water, period. Those who'd fallen asleep (or passed out drunk?) after lunch had to put on their uniforms over sweaty, sand-coated, itchy bodies and fly that way for the next six hours. Few pilots made that mistake more than once. Eventually, gradual improvements in tourist facilities saw our rudimentary stone hotel with its insect-infested rooms evolve into a Caribbean-style luxury resort complete with imported palm trees. Frankly, once I'd learned to deal with the water shutdowns I preferred the original version.

It rarely rained on Sal, but when it did, it poured. We were coming in to land on just such a night. The ILS was behaving erratically because of the unusual weather, so the approach had to be flown manually. The co-pilot, who was flying the sector (captain and co-pilot generally took turns to fly each leg), decided to go around and try again. His first two attempts failed. We now had just enough fuel for one more try. If that didn't work we'd have to head for our alternate airport at Las Palmas, in the Canary Islands.

We'd still have had to come back to Sal after that, so it would have meant a long night's flying.

The normally languid tone of the Sal tower controller sounded strained as he cleared us for the approach. At 500 feet AGL we saw the runway but were not well positioned to land on it. The captain, a short, volatile fellow with a habitually foul mouth, yelled, 'I've got it,' grabbed the controls from the co-pilot and literally manhandled the jet onto the runway. It was impressive flying but lousy airmanship. The co-pilot sulked all the way to the hotel.

Then there were the dogs. Sal was overrun by wild canines. Periodically, the Verdeans would get fed up with them and have a dog purge. This would thin out their numbers for a few months but never succeeded in wiping them all out.

One of the dogs' favourite hangouts was the airport; they particularly loved the apron, sitting under the fuselage of parked aircraft. Despite the warm tropical climate, they'd gather under the hot air outlet from the air conditioning units or sit close to the hot brake assemblies. To get a prime basking spot, the dogs would rush out while our jet was still taxiing in. Somehow, they seemed to know in advance which parking spot we'd been assigned on the wide concrete apron. Some cut it too close, which meant that three-legged dogs were a common sight among the airport pack. Eventually, we learned just to follow the slower three-legged dogs and the cabin crew learned to follow the pilots. It made sense in a Sal kind of way.

Chapter 11
Deadly Navigation

It took the end of the Cold War for investigators to learn the full story of what happened to Flight KAL007. The Korean Air Lines passenger plane was shot down by a Soviet fighter jet for straying into Soviet airspace in 1983. All 269 SOB (souls on board), the total number of people on the flight, were killed, and the fallout from the incident triggered enough tension between Washington and Moscow to raise fears of actual conflict.

Reading the official report years later was a disturbing experience. I realised how close one of my own flights as a boy pilot had come to experiencing a similar navigational disaster.

There are many different reasons for having to change course when you're on a flight.

Once a pilot selects NAV (navigation) mode on the autopilot, an aircraft will follow a preprogrammed route all the way to the destination, but this doesn't avoid problems such as thunderstorms in the flight path. Thunderstorms are sometimes strong enough to destroy an aircraft, so we have a dedicated weather radar system to help avoid them. That's easy enough when it comes to individual thunderstorm cells. However, the cells often develop in a line along a weather front that can stretch for hundreds of miles. In order to cross the front, we might have to fly along the line until we find a gap between two cells and dart through it.

To do so, the pilot has to change from NAV to HDG (heading) mode and steer around a thunderstorm by twirling the heading knob. It's very unusual to do a long-range flight and never have to turn off track to avoid thunderstorms. In fact, I never experienced that luxury until I flew over the frozen polar regions where, due to the intense cold, there are no thunderstorms and thus no weather to avoid.

As a co-pilot, though, I often had to modify my dealings with weather to accommodate the quirks of some of our captains. Airline pilots are a conservative and cautious group, neither risk-takers nor overly nervous in the cockpit. But I twice flew with particularly nervous SAA captains, both of whom had inexplicably developed a strong fear of flying in clouds.

With one of them, I was flying a Boeing 727 in a solid overcast with embedded thunderstorms, a daily experience in airline flying. As there was zero outside visibility, we were using the weather radar to avoid the cumulonimbus cells. The captain became so agitated that he actually switched off the radar, the very instrument you need to track thunderstorms. Then he got up and disappeared into the bathroom. The flight engineer and I looked at each other in stunned amazement. I switched the radar back on and continued to avoid the embedded cells. The captain returned, sat down and resumed command as if nothing had happened. Amazing what a quick trip to the loo can do.

The second time was on a 747 with a captain nicknamed 'Blip' for his habit of diverting off track for the tiniest blip (return) on the weather radar. Avoiding thunderstorms is one thing; trying to avoid clouds is another. He took us so far off course in avoiding clouds while flying south over Italy that the exasperated controller demanded to know our true intentions, and transferred us to a control area that we'd never entered before. By the time we got back on track, Blip had wasted 30 minutes of fuel and upset Italian ATC for no good reason.

Then there was the time I flew with a senior captain nicknamed 'Avbob' (after the funeral society) for his gloomy demeanour. SAA had been granted a new departure slot out of Manchester, so a flight engineer and I had travelled by coach from London to crew the first flight.

It was an exercise in obstructive bureaucracy right from the start, with the entire crew being made to haul their luggage off the bus at the airport entry gate for a security check, repack it and then unpack it again at the terminal.

But the bigger problem was that we weren't taken to a dispatch office for a briefing – a mistake at an unfamiliar airport. Instead, we self-briefed from the flight documents the SAA agent brought to the aircraft. Unnoticed by us was the fact that our route briefly crossed into one of the seven Oceanic Control Areas of the North Atlantic Region, something we'd never done before.

The route between Europe and North America is one of the busiest airspaces in the world and is controlled by very strict routing and entry points in the Oceanic Area. No aircraft can enter this region without obtaining prior clearance specifying the entry point, time of entry, altitude, speed and exact route through the region.

We took off from Manchester knowing nothing of this procedure.

The flight proceeded normally until five minutes before the Oceanic entry point. The controller called us and asked if we'd already obtained our Oceanic clearance. I didn't know what he was talking about so I said no, where could we get it?

The ATC controller went nuts. He verbally rebuked me and gave me a frequency to call immediately.

If Manchester ATC was angry, Oceanic Control was furious.

'You should have called for clearance 20 minutes ago,' the controller spat. 'You may not enter the region till you have it. You must hold (circle) outside the region.'

The day was going from bad to worse. Holding in a long-range airliner, with its carefully calculated fuel load, can mean not having enough fuel to reach your destination – and we were just about to hit the Oceanic crossing point.

Instead of holding, I advised the controller that we were going to follow the Oceanic boundary southward, and could they give us an entry point further down range?

We were deep into uncharted territory here. For all we knew, we were committing a new 'crime' to compound our original sin. We could easily be ordered back to Manchester.

After a short hesitation, the Oceanic controller, stunned by our latest move, asked, 'Springbok, have you ever been here before?' I admitted that it was our first flight and we had been improperly briefed. Could he help us out?

'Well,' he mused, 'I think the lesson has been learned.' He gave us an en route entry point at a suitable time.

I leaned back in my seat, coated with screw-up sweat, and sighed with relief. Then I noticed that Avbob was looking amazingly calm. He hadn't said a word throughout the exchange, and I realised he probably didn't have the faintest idea what had just transpired. He was just looking out of the window, ignoring the radio chatter and dreaming of his pension, I guess.

The navigation problems of the ill-fated KAL007 – and my own brush with them in SAA – had a different cause. In our case, we'd taken off in an easterly direction from Mauritius for Perth, Australia. By then, inertial navigation systems (INS), developed during the space race and as guidance for military missiles, were standard equipment on long-range airliners. INS offered a self-contained system to calculate the position of an aircraft without the need for external sources such as ground stations. (Interestingly, the US defence establishment was so worried about making such an accurate guidance platform available to potential enemies that early INS systems included a built-in error to prevent it being too precise. A couple of miles off is nothing in long-range airline navigation but means a complete miss when targeting a building or missile silo. Later, as GPS and other systems began providing pinpoint accuracy to civilian users, the inbuilt error became irrelevant and was removed from the system.)

INS is essentially a gyro-stabilised platform exquisitely sensitive to acceleration forces. It calculates your position by measuring those forces to determine your movement from a known latitude and longitude. Because pilots could easily input the necessary data, the system quickly made human navigators obsolete.

On my particular flight, we were slightly to the right of the INS route to the first waypoint en route to Australia. The co-pilot, who was flying that sector, turned us a few degrees left to intercept the track as soon as we got clearance from ATC. Then he turned the navigation mode selector to INS to allow the autopilot to intercept and automatically follow the inertial route to Perth.

Except it never happened. A northerly wind had sprung up and it held our 747 to the right of the required track. Unfortunately, no one noticed that the navigation system hadn't yet captured – locked on to – the inertial track when we passed the first waypoint. With such sensitive equipment, small errors are quickly magnified. Once we passed it, the track to the next few waypoints turned progressively left, making it impossible to intercept off our current heading. Worse, passing abeam a waypoint makes the INS click over to the next leg as if you've passed directly over the point, so at a cursory glance the INS display looks normal.

This was a remote area over open ocean and there was no radar coverage to alert air traffic controllers to our growing error. They simply assumed we were on track. So did we.

Hours later, I was sitting in the captain's seat doing regular relief duties when a single amber light on the forward panel caught my eye. It bothered me because there should be no amber lights in normal flight; they should either be green or off. I stared at the amber until I understood what it was telling me: that the NAV mode was still armed because we had not yet captured the track. I was stunned when I turned the data knob on the INS to see what was going on. It showed a track error of 160 nautical miles. That meant we were 160 miles off course and still deviating.

I nudged the co-pilot and quietly brought the error to his attention. He looked puzzled, then went pale as he saw what had happened. After looking at a chart, he locked the INS onto a distant waypoint. The amber light instantly turned green.

We were too far off course to recover our original track, so he headed to a point about an hour ahead and flew the correct track from there on. I didn't mention it again. Nor did the co-pilot, who ultimately was to blame for the error. But if anything had happened to us on that flight, no one would have searched that far off track. Our aircraft would simply have disappeared and we'd have become another unsolved aviation mystery.

I might have forgotten about it myself had it not been for the tragedy of KAL007. That Korean Air Lines 747 had strayed more than 200 miles from its scheduled route from Anchorage to Seoul when it was shot down by two air-to-air missiles near Russia's Sakhalin Island on 1 September 1983. It crashed into the sea about 30 miles from the island. Moscow claimed that the plane was on a spying mission for the United States. US President Ronald Reagan called it 'an act of barbarism'.

The big question, though, was why the Korean plane had gone so far off course. The International Civil Aviation Organization (ICAO), an agency of the United Nations, could not find a definitive answer without the plane's 'black box', or flight recorders, which the Soviets had found a month after the crash – but had kept secret. ICAO's interim findings suggested two theories attributing the deviation to human error with the navigation system. One, according to the report, was that the autopilot mode selector was inadvertently left in HDG mode, which meant that the flight path was not adjusted to calculate deviations that would have been caused by the wind at the aircraft's flight altitude – typically up to 41 000 feet. The winds at those levels can affect an aircraft's heading, so not factoring them in would have allowed the INS to indicate waypoint passage despite not being on the assigned track. The second theory was that one of the pilots had incorrectly entered a ten-degree error in longitude.

In 1992, months after the collapse of the Soviet Union, Russia's President Boris Yeltsin agreed to hand over tapes from the recovered cockpit voice recorder and digital flight data recorder. This enabled ICAO to issue its final report. It supported the 'heading mode' theory, noting that the crew's failure to detect the aircraft's deviation 'indicated a lack of situational awareness and flight deck coordination on the part of the crew'.

It was precisely the same operational error we had made; both aircraft were flying a constant heading instead of following the INS track. In the empty southern Indian Ocean, we had got away with it. On the sensitive Northern Pacific (NOPAC) route system, they hadn't.

One further weird coincidence? When I joined Nippon Cargo Airlines years later, I routinely departed from Anchorage on the identical NOPAC route that KAL007 was supposed to follow – but didn't.

Chapter 12
Seat Sex and Men's Clubs

Forget the legendary 'mile-high' club of sex in aircraft bathrooms. Most onboard sex takes place right on the passenger seats. It wasn't unusual for the cabin interphone to ding in the cockpit with a call from a giggling air hostess asking us what to do about a couple having noisy seat sex. We usually told them it was best to just throw a few blankets over the couple and let them finish.

I once inadvertently witnessed seat sex between strangers when I was travelling in first class from London to Cape Town. The pair across the aisle were cordial and polite before takeoff, chatty over drinks, BFFs over dinner and staring meaningfully at each other over dessert. As the alcohol flowed, it was patently clear what was going to happen after the lights went out.

And happen it did, watched by a young boy sitting in front of them who'd wedged his head between two seats to stare enthralled at the proceedings. When the new day dawned, the once-jovial couple could barely find a word to say to each other. After breakfast, they turned in opposite directions and dozed, to the disappointment of the boy, who undoubtedly was hoping for an encore.

In Johannesburg, the guy disappeared without even saying goodbye. The woman and I both flew on to Cape Town where she fell into the loving arms of her husband.

Meanwhile, bad crew behaviour also wasn't confined to drinking. When I joined SAA as a young single man, it was common for the older pilots to have air hostess girlfriends. So common, in fact, that they were called 'airline wives'. It was clear that some of the younger women saw a married pilot-boyfriend as a sort of power fashion accessory. They knew that the relationship was unlikely to lead anywhere, but they felt it gave them special status among the aircrew and on the aircraft. The guys, of course, were only too happy to go along.

Mostly, I tried to avoid passing judgement. It was a different era and a different workplace culture. SAA then was the ultimate boys' club. Those of us flying the plane were all men – career professionals who'd almost all come through the air force. The air hostesses, on the other hand, were mostly young women who'd joined the airline for the adventure of seeing the world for a few years before moving on. The airline rarely took older women anyway; it wanted attractive youngsters who looked good in their designer uniforms. These women were expected to maintain a certain weight during their employment and were trained to wear their hair and make-up in a prescribed style. (The male flight attendants, then known as air stewards, were more likely to see a long-term future with the airline but there tended to be little socialising between pilots and stewards.)

Obviously, not all the women wanted the attention. I remember one international trip when a junior air hostess hung around with me for protection after a much-disliked captain kept pestering her. He wasn't her boss – cockpit and cabin crews had separate reporting lines and managers – so in the end it was me who got written up in his report when we returned to Johannesburg. 'This Boy Pilot thinks the airline is there to take him from one party to another,' he wrote. 'He has zero command potential.'

I had to smile when the pool manager called me in for comment. I thought it was the perfect description of the boy pilot's job. But aside from the captain's obvious spite, my record showed that I'd displayed plenty of command potential when I'd been selected as an air force Dakota commander at 20. The manager agreed and threw the report into File 13, also known as the rubbish bin.

Seat Sex and Men's Clubs

One of the times I felt moral outrage was when I flew into London with a devout Afrikaans-speaking pilot, an official of his church. This pilot had once put a personal note into my box inviting me to come and pray with him and his wife. No doubt he wanted to excise my Jewish devils. But on that UK trip he didn't even make it to the hotel; we all saw his English girlfriend waiting at the airport to meet him, and then we didn't see him again until our return flight. I guess he was excising her devils as well.

Sometimes these relationships lasted for years. The pilot would live at home with his wife between trips and arrange his schedule to go on flights with his airline wife. Some pilots would go a step further, packing their bags for what they told their wife was a trip abroad and then heading off to spend the week at their girlfriend's place in another part of town. Few even tried to keep these relationships quiet on our trips. I remember my wife, Arlene, watching in disgust as a pilot passionately kissed his girlfriend goodbye in the lobby of a Durban hotel – then waited in the same spot to give an almost-as-passionate greeting to his wife when she arrived on a visit from Johannesburg a few minutes later.

In theory, air-hostess girlfriends avoided the flights when the captain was on a planned trip with his wife. Sometimes, though, if a wife spontaneously decided to go on a trip that had already been arranged with the airline wife, say over Christmas, then the result was worthy of a Broadway farce.

I was on one such trip with both women on board. The captain was a nervous wreck right from the start. His airline wife cut him no slack. She berated him mercilessly for ruining the trip every time she saw him, including in the cockpit. His actual wife sat quietly in first class saying nothing – presumably because she knew she'd trumped them both.

The whole crew gathered at a restaurant for Christmas lunch. The normally garrulous captain and his wife sat at one end of the table, his face a picture of anxiety while his airline *amour* fumed at the other end. She drank too quickly, laughed too loud and finally stormed out in tears.

It was fine entertainment for everyone there, but invariably these situations ended in tears or divorce. Many pilots were on their third or fourth wives. One fellow had married so many times he was known as the 'floating trophy'.

Towards the end of my boy pilot days, a new order started demanding a higher level of professionalism from the crews. It wasn't enough to end all of the old habits, of course.

On one flight to London, a check captain was sitting in the jump seat to conduct an annual in-flight test on the captain in command of the plane. As we started to push back from the terminal, the commanding captain turned to face his crew. Instead of giving the expected takeoff briefing, he told a filthy joke about airline pilots.

The crew exploded with laughter, none more so than the captain who'd told the joke. The checker, who was much younger than the captain, sat and fumed.

Later in the flight, the captain invited some attractive women passengers to visit the cockpit – not an unusual thing in the pre-9/11 years. He sat half out of his seat, entertaining them with his stories as he draped himself across the centre console – not a good idea seeing as this is where radio selectors and other critical controls are located, instruments that would be dangerous to knock out of place in flight.

The checker, whose role is to evaluate a pilot's performance and proficiency, watched it all, saying nothing.

When we landed, the checker pulled the captain aside for a private chat. He emerged a changed, unhappy man. At our hotel, he called a crew meeting and berated us for acting so unprofessionally on the aircraft. Things would be different on the next sector, he promised. So watch out! He then went to his room to drink away his *uitkak* (rebuke).

And indeed things were different on the next leg. For a couple of hours. We all sat quietly in the darkened cockpit until an air hostess he knew came to visit him. Ten minutes later he was half out of his seat, draped across the centre console, telling her another filthy joke. The flight progressed as usual after that.

There were a few raunchy adventures on the ground too.

One of our favourite crew haunts in Lisbon was the Texas Bar. It was located downtown in what is now a trendy street painted pink but in those days was still the city's rough red-light district, full of prostitutes and sailors coming to find them from the nearby docks.

We didn't partake of the fleshy offerings but liked the bar's grungy atmosphere and cheap drinks. One evening, when we were dancing on the little dance floor with some of the air hostesses we'd taken there, I felt a searing pain in my left buttock. I looked around and saw a prostitute furtively walking away. Then I saw her jab a long bloody needle into an air hostess's backside. She was clearly upset that all the women we'd brought in might distract her potential clients, so we cleared off rather than risk getting pricked again.

A few years later, as the Aids pandemic took hold across the world, I worried about whether I could have been infected by that communal needle in the bum. Luckily not – the Texas Bar always did have a better class of prostitute.

On another trip to Portugal, I talked the flight engineer into hiring a car with me for a couple of days. We managed to keep our vehicle rentals to a reasonable cost because we'd mastered the art of disconnecting the speedometer for much of the journey to keep our mileage charges down. (We also routinely manipulated the TV boxes in our hotel rooms to watch pay movies for free.)

We headed inland towards the Portuguese/Spanish border to

explore the fortified medieval towns and villages that dotted the once hotly contested area but were now sleepy backwaters. Evening found us in one of these walled towns enjoying dinner at a small local eatery.

We didn't speak Portuguese, but I was able to use the Spanish I'd taught myself from a tape-and-book course to explain to the rotund owner that we were foreign aircrew and needed rooms for the night. He then picked up the phone and within a few moments had it all arranged. After quite a few celebratory drinks with him, we followed him to a large dilapidated-looking hotel.

We were shown (by the same guy!) to a large, dusty room that had clearly not been used for quite some time. It looked like the two of us were expected to share the room, but we were okay with that. What we weren't okay with was being set up or robbed, something that was always in the back of our minds. So when he told us he'd like to show us something special in the town, we were both instantly on our guard.

But as there were two of us, both healthy young males and full of wine, we followed him into the dark back streets.

He led us down one of the narrow, twisting cobbled streets so typical of a Portuguese hilltop town, stopping at a stone building with a shuttered metal grate. He pulled up the grate with a flourish and knocked on the heavy wooden door behind it. The area looked deserted and we were now sorry we'd agreed to this stupidity. The door opened instantly.

A neatly dressed young man in a waiter's jacket greeted the restaurant owner by name. He nodded and slipped past the young man into the building. We followed, against our better judgement. It turned out to be one of the most unusual places I've ever seen.

The passageway was lined with dark wood and led to a large, softly lit stone chamber with huge wine vats set against the walls. White-jacketed waiters were tapping dark wine from the barrels and hurrying to serve it in silver jugs to a group of elegantly dressed men standing in the centre of the room. We instantly felt underdressed in our travelling jeans.

The local mayor was there, our host pointed out, along with the police chief, bank manager, important businessmen, landowners and now us, specially invited guests.

I asked the restaurant owner why there were no women in the place, neither serving nor as guests. 'But this is the town's secret men's club,' he exclaimed. 'Where men come to drink at night or just to get away from their wives or families. Why would we allow women in here?' I must say, I saw his point.

Two other things instantly caught my eye.

One was that there were cobwebs everywhere. Not little spider webs in the corners but great big sheets of the stuff that hung eerily from ceiling to floor, covering the walls in some areas. I couldn't imagine the size of the spiders that created these mega-webs. Some moved gently in the breeze of a ceiling fan or actually brushed over you when you walked. I was proudly told the webs had never been touched in hundreds of years, something that was easy to believe.

The other interesting thing was on high shelves that circled the chamber. They held a mixture of soft-porn pictures and sex toys such as large rubber penises. Such things were freely available in Europe and hardly shocking to most Europeans, of course, but Portugal still had a deeply religious, conservative culture, especially outside the big cities. As such, these *objets d'sex* were edgy, scandalous goods to the residents of this small mountain town. Our host proudly pointed them out one by one.

We sampled a glass or two of different wines from the barrels and were then introduced to the mayor, who clearly wasn't that pleased to see us there. I guess we looked like we didn't belong, especially in jeans. I got the feeling that our host was going to get a serious lecture the next day about the sanctity of their men's club. The mayor did tell us about some local caves that we should try to see. We were then politely shown the door.

We headed to the caves after a large breakfast at our new friend's place. He was nowhere in sight, maybe still sleeping it off. We paid the entry fee and were led down to a large, dripping cavern carved out of limestone. It was filled with stalactite columns, similar to South Africa's vast Cango Caves, near Oudtshoorn. Unfortunately, they'd lit the cave with hundreds of coloured lights, which destroyed its natural tranquillity and gave it a garish, disco-like atmosphere. But at least there were no giant spiders. Or rubber penises.

Chapter 13
Dead Man's Shoes

Like most airlines, SAA was a 'dead man's shoes' outfit. There was no set time to serve in a particular position; promotion occurred only when a slot became available and was awarded strictly by seniority based on your date of hire. The rate of promotion depended on airline expansion, increasing route structure, frequency of flights and senior captain retirements.

Due to increasingly strict international sanctions against apartheid, SAA was going in the wrong direction. Our world was shrinking and promotion was so slow that the first thing we did if we heard of a pilot having a serious accident was to check his position on the seniority list. If he was junior, the accident was a tragedy. If he was senior, it was an opportunity.

After two years as boy pilot, my number finally came up in 1981 and I was assigned to a Boeing 727 co-pilot course. I would finally be flying again, instead of watching old farts fly.

The 727, a three-engine short-range jet, was at that time being gradually phased out of SAA service in favour of the more economical Boeing 737. In fact, I would fly the 727 for only a year before the airline ceased operating the type and sold off the aircraft. The 727 was a pilot's aircraft, easy to fly, with few vices – and such incredible performance that pilots nicknamed it the 'three-hole orgasmatron'.

I reported for the 727 course in Johannesburg. It began with six weeks of ground school and exams on Aircraft Technical, 727 Performance and Emergency Equipment. Then we used SAA's 727 flight simulator for some basic procedural training. Unfortunately, the aging 727 simulator was barely functional, but rather than paying to fix it, SAA elected to buy simulator time at another facility – a common practice in the airline industry.

We were sent to a United Airlines hub in Denver, Colorado, for our real simulator training. When you hire another airline's simulator, you get to use it at the hours they're not interested in using it themselves, usually from midnight to 6 am. Those early hours were tiresome, but I took the sessions seriously and it went well. We finished our training earlier than expected and ended up with a few days free, so we decided to do some sightseeing. We hired a huge 1960s car – a proverbial land yacht – from an outfit called Rent a Lemon. Before we drove off, they poured in a gallon of oil and another of transmission fluid. The car's fuel consumption was outrageous but at the time petrol was very cheap in this part of the world.

Our first stop was at the local mall for lunch. We parked in the sprawling lot and one of the flight engineers noticed a woman's head bobbing between cars a few rows away.

'Perhaps she's fixing a flat tyre?' he wondered out loud.

South African males are very helpful, so we walked over to see if we could help her with the tyre.

But the woman didn't have a tyre problem. She had a morning drinking problem and was squatting down to urinate. She went wild when we suddenly appeared next to her, offering to help. We ran into the mall with her drunken screams of 'filthy perverts' echoing across the parking lot.

The rest of the trip went better. We drove our land yacht from town to town for two days, winding into the majestic Rocky Mountains before finally turning back at Climax, which at more than 11 000 feet above sea level was once the highest settlement in the United States. Coloradans claim it's technically not a ghost town, but when all that's left is a mine that once produced more than 75 per cent of the world's molybdenum – a mineral used to harden steel, among other things – you could have fooled us. More importantly, we were pleased that the town's name suggested we weren't the only perverts in Colorado.

Our next stop on the conversion trail was flying training, where my training partner and I screwed up right from the start.

Our instructor had left a message for us to meet him in Room 5 at 8 am for a preflight briefing.

At 8 sharp, we were already waiting in Lecture Room 5.

By 8.30, he still hadn't arrived and we were getting worried. We asked around and discovered flight briefings were not done in the regular classrooms. The flight instructors' rooms were on a different floor!

We rushed upstairs and found a furious instructor about to leave Briefing Room 5.

We apologised profusely and explained our mistake. We must have looked convincingly stupid because he sat down again and briefed us on our flying training schedule. An hour later, we closed the entry door of a fuelled but otherwise completely empty 727. We were heading out for two hours of flying, followed by circuits and landings.

The 727 was a magnificent machine, designed and built in an era when fuel economy was not a major consideration. It had three engines when two would have done, and was overbuilt in many other respects. Other great features were nose-wheel brakes, in addition to main-wheel brakes, and the most effective speed brakes of any current, past or probably future airliner. It also had a three-man crew, something that was rapidly being phased out on more modern airliners.

The aircraft was easy to fly but tricky to land, as the main wheels were well aft of the centre of gravity. Thus a normal flare technique would cause you to drive the main wheels onto the runway for a hard landing. What was needed was a 'roll-on' technique, a slight

105

push on the control column before touchdown after executing a normal flare. Without that extra step, every 727 landing would be a hard landing, but once you mastered the roll-on technique, it could be used on all Boeing types to soften the touchdown.

I must confess that initially I had some trouble 'finding the ground' (determining height from the runway). Just like on Harvards, I was a slow learner when it came to landing 727s. Once I hit the ground so hard that all the passenger oxygen masks dropped from the overhead bustle and a cockpit alarm went off. After a few more weeks that included more flight training, a flight check, a number of route training sectors with an instructor and finally a line check – a check ride where an examiner sits in the cockpit watching every aspect of your performance from ground briefings to taxiing on a regular passenger-carrying sector – South Africa's civil aviation authority endorsed my licence so I could fly the line as a 727 co-pilot.

My education on 727s didn't end there. I returned to Denver six months later for my biannual simulator check. My first visit had been the beginning of my airline co-pilot career; the second would see the end of a captain's career.

I was scheduled to do my check with a seasoned captain nicknamed 'Loop en Val' (walk and fall) for his curious stumbling gait. He wasn't a skilful pilot but had managed to hold on to his flying licence until drink got the better of him. This time around, the simulator check was an excuse for a firing session – unfortunately with me in the co-pilot's seat.

Loop en Val was an airline legend. He rolled his own cigarettes from vile pouch tobacco with little seeds in the mix – and he could roll them with one hand while flying a 727 with the other. When things got too busy, he would stick his homemade cigarette to the windscreen with a little spit. Popping flare-ups punctuated the air as each seed ignited. He seemed impervious to cold, wearing a short-sleeved shirt throughout winter. And he was so strong that he reputedly once ripped a 727 speed brake lever right out of its housing.

But he had long since ceased to cope with his captain's duties. After countless warnings, SAA was giving him one last chance to pass a simulator check.

My enduring memory of that check was the smokescreen that enveloped us when *Loop en Val* lit up in the simulator. Early in the session, he pulled out the first of three home-rolled smokes from the top pocket of his shirt and lit it with a visibly shaking hand. The thick, grey smoke from his black tobacco was bad enough in an air-conditioned cockpit. In an enclosed simulator it created such a smoggy haze that I found it difficult to see the flight instruments in front of my face without leaning well forward.

Loop en Val chain-smoked all three, cooking his own goose in the process. The check went very badly and he was forced to retire. Unfortunately, it would take quite a number of years before the revolting habit of cockpit smoking went the same way.

When I joined the SAAF, and later SAA, many pilots were heavy smokers. It was part of the fly hard, play even harder culture. There was no consideration at all for non-smokers, and pilots smoked whenever they wished in the confined cockpit space. Unlike to-day, the right to smoke in the enclosed cockpit trumped any other rights. In addition, smoking was a taboo subject, not open for serious discussion.

If there were three smokers on an overseas flight, one of whom might have a pipe, the whole cockpit became wreathed in a foul grey miasma. In fact, some pilots childishly increased their smoking rate to torment non-smokers.

It was barely any better in the passenger cabin. Planes were divided into farcical smoking and non-smoking sections. The smoking section started a row behind the non-smoking seats, with no physical barrier separating them. The entire plane stank of smoke. Non-smokers on crowded flights often had no choice but to sit in smoking seats. Smokers would light up wherever they were. This wasn't just an SAA problem. I once took a flight on Olympic Airlines, then still Greece's national carrier, and someone blatantly lit up in the non-smoking section. I pressed the attendant-call button to complain, and the offending smoker got up and came over to my seat. He was the steward!

Things started to change as public attitudes towards second-hand smoke hardened. Cabin crew were unhappy about being constantly exposed to passengers' smoke. The habit was also costly: tobacco smoke left a tarry, sticky residue on aircraft systems, valves and instruments that was expensive to remove – if it could be removed at all. And there was the ever-present danger of fire, especially when people smoked in the bathrooms.

Eventually the day came and in 1987 SAA banned smoking on all its internal flights, one of the first airlines in the world to do so. Smoking would still be allowed on international flights until it was stopped by international agreement – but not for another decade.

Meanwhile nothing changed for us. Pilots continued to smoke in the cockpit.

I hate smoking. My father was a lifelong smoker and the sight of his reddened face and hacking cough put me off tobacco for life. He used to smoke in the car with the windows closed, and I remember my frustration at being stuck in the smoky atmosphere.

I decided to try doing something about the cockpit smoking without criticising or antagonising my smoking colleagues. I wanted to show them that smoking in the cockpit was bad airmanship even if they didn't care what it did to their health.

I had previously researched and written a long article titled 'Physiological effects of smoking on a pilot' in conjunction with a professor at Wits University. It examined the short-term effects of smoking in a reduced-oxygen environment, such as an airliner flying at high altitude.

The results were quite stunning. The evidence I found indicated that a smoker's impaired ventilation efficiency meant that three cigarettes an hour could cause more cognitive and reactive impairment at high altitude than drinking a unit of alcohol, a slowdown to well under the minimum acceptable level for a pilot. And many pilots smoked more than three an hour. My conclusion was that someone who smoked heavily in the cockpit would do better to have a drink, as smokers' responses were dangerously slowed and their minds were on autopilot.

I offered the article to our pilots' union for publication. They ran it with a weasel warning that it wasn't their own opinion.

All hell broke loose. Besides the usual 'fucking Jew' comments, I was warned by quite a few smoking captains what would happen when they flew with me: they would smoke their lungs out to spite me. But they got over it. In the end, the healthier lifestyles of modern pilots made cockpit smoking a moot problem. Most pilots, with a few holdouts, stopped smoking completely. And everyone stopped smoking in the cockpit.

It rapidly became the exception to climb into a 747 cockpit still foul with the stench of all-night smoking from the previous crew. Along with the Royal Family, it was one of the things from the past that I didn't miss at all.

Chapter 14
Passengers at 30 000 Feet

Before the attacks of 9/11 changed aviation security, we usually flew with the cockpit door wide open. Some captains went further and issued general invitations over the passenger announcement (PA) system for passengers to visit the flight deck.

It was good public relations and helped make nights pass a little quicker for us. Children were always particularly good visitors, but adults could be obnoxious know-it-alls – especially when they arrived drunk.

They entered the cockpit reeking of booze, breathed all over us and left an alcohol trail in their wake.

Sometimes the cabin staff would call us to complain that a noisy, drunken party had started in the cabin, particularly when there was a sports team or their supporters on board.

Luckily, we had a solution for that.

The engineer would slowly raise the cabin altitude on the pressurisation system, reducing the oxygen supply to the already oxygen-deficient drinkers to induce them to calm down and go to sleep. In addition, he would lower the cabin temperature to make them less active.

It rarely failed. Within an hour, everyone in the cabin would be asleep. The occasional cost was having to give supplementary oxygen to a couple of elderly folk, but the cabin staff never complained about that.

As pilots, we tended not to deal directly with passengers; we typically only got involved when the cabin crew needed our help.

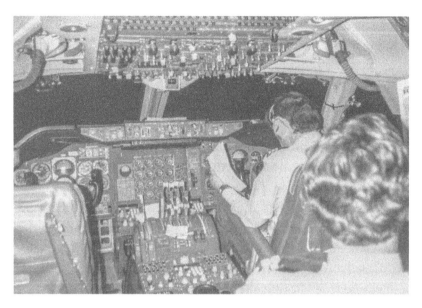

A visitor's view of the cockpit

But when they weren't drunk or difficult, the passengers sometimes gave us a good laugh.

On one occasion, we'd landed in East London on a turnaround and were waiting on the apron for our new passengers to arrive for what we'd been told was a completely full flight to Johannesburg.

To our amazement, a long line of black passengers began to stream out of the terminal. A big soap company had held a national sales competition for their thousands of staff. The prize was a flight to Johannesburg and a paid two-day conference/holiday.

This was 1983, when South African beaches, suburbs, schools, restaurants, theatres, buses, trains – pretty much everything you could think of – were still segregated by race. Only whites were hired as SAA pilots or cabin staff. However, the airline was one of the few places that passengers of all races were allowed to travel together, probably because air travel was governed by international regulations.

The lucky local winners, many from rural areas, were happy and excited as they boarded. They were also loud. It was clear that few had flown before – most black South Africans could not afford an air ticket – and, unfamiliar with sit-down-and-be-quiet flying etiquette, they exuberantly chatted and laughed at full volume across the cabin. Some danced down the aisle.

The cabin staff were red in the face and sweating in their efforts to restore some kind of order. (From what I could hear them saying, it was clear they were also secretly appalled at having to serve black people.)

Into this bedlam walked a prim white passenger, a middle-aged Afrikaans woman dressed in her Sunday best. She entered the plane, took one look into the cabin and stopped dead in her tracks. She turned to the cabin chief and asked in a low urgent voice: 'Is ek op die verkeerde vliegtuig?' (Am I on the wrong plane?)

Weirdly, some passengers actually thought they had some say in what we were doing.

One Tuesday afternoon in my 727 days, we'd taken off from Cape Town and were heading to Johannesburg via Bloemfontein. Once we were in the cruise, the captain picked up the PA and briefed the passengers on our altitude, landing time in Bloemfontein and the usual useless facts about our flight.

The cabin chief walked into the open cockpit and reported that some passengers were saying the flight was supposed to be going to Kimberley, not Bloemfontein.

The flight log distinctly showed Bloemfontein as our destination, but mistakes are always possible. We were already out of radio range of our Cape Town office, so the captain told the cabin crew chief to take a vote among the passengers to see how many thought we were going to Kimberley and how many to Bloemfontein. The vote was tallied and the winner was Kimberley by a nose.

We informed ATC of our new destination.

Passengers at 30 000 Feet

We landed in Kimberley, taxied to our usual parking spot and shut down. The ground engineer came on board and greeted us: 'Nice to see you, but why are you here? We don't have a flight from Cape Town on a Tuesday.' The next stop we made was in Bloemfontein. It made our day a little longer, but everyone seemed happier.

On more routine flights – when we knew where we were going – we found other ways to amuse ourselves. One of our favourite diversions was nose-wheel roulette, a betting game that was easy to play with five crew members (two in the cockpit, three in the cabin) and five flight legs a day.

Every co-pilot carried a piece of chalk or soap in his pocket. On the day's first walk-around for an exterior inspection of the plane, he would use the chalk or soap to divide one of the nose-wheel tyres into five equal-size numbered sections. A cabin crew member would later inspect his handiwork – this was serious business.

The bet was normally one rand per sector and each crew member would choose a number for the day, one through five. On shutdown at each destination, the number at the bottom of the wheel touching the tarmac was the winner.

One problem with this game was that if it was wet, the numbers would often wash off. Another problem was that some pilots found a way to cheat.

They started their nefarious tricks after we taxied in and came to a stop, when a ground engineer would establish contact with the cockpit by plugging his headset into a nose-wheel socket. Before shutting the engines down, the cheating pilot would ask the ground engineer which number was touching the tarmac. He would then roll the aircraft slowly forward to his own number.

Cabin crew eventually got wise to this trick because they could see the jet was slightly forward of the stop line whenever that particular pilot won. But what ended it for good was when a frequent passenger asked to join the nose-wheel roulette game. That was game over.

Overall, though, I have to confess that we didn't always think much about passenger comfort when we were flying.

Most captains followed most of the rules most of the time, but some were cowboy pilots who followed no rules whatsoever. The only SOPs they observed were the jet's maximum limits on things like speed, altitude or performance, which they pushed every time they flew. Luckily, the 727 was a very tough aircraft and as long as there were no serious incidents and they flew normally on check rides, no one really tried to stop them or, indeed, seemed to care.

Unfortunately for those seated in the back, cowboy flyers saw passenger comfort not as a consideration but as an impediment. Passengers most likely to bear the brunt of this were those on the Kimberley–Bloemfontein and Port Elizabeth–East London sectors. Both were short legs and there was ongoing competition to see who could fly them in the shortest time.

You only stood a chance of a record time if you were taking off and landing in the same direction as the flight track. Even a 90-degree turn after takeoff or for landing simply took too long. Most takeoffs are at a reduced thrust setting to save fuel and engine wear, but to make a serious attempt at the record you had to use full thrust for takeoff, irrespective of weight.

The clock started on brake release. You got airborne, held the 727 in a very slow climb and raised the landing gear. As the speed quickly increased, flaps were raised in a continuous movement. It was sometimes possible to be clean (flaps up) before you passed the end of the runway.

The slow climb was maintained until the speed was on the clackers (maximum speed warning horn). You then climbed on the clackers. It goes without saying that cruise was on the clackers. Top of climb (TOC) and top of descent (TOD) often came within moments of each other. Descent was on the clackers until 12 miles on a straight-in approach with the speed about 365 knots indicated air speed (IAS).

Then you closed the thrust levers and pulled maximum speed brake. This was where the 727's speed brake excelled. The fierce deceleration pushed us hard against the shoulder straps. As the speed decayed, flaps were run in a continuous stream, landing gear was dropped and the speed brake was stowed.

When perfectly executed, you'd stabilise with thrust at 500 feet and land shortly thereafter. The clock stopped when you turned off the runway. We didn't factor in the time it took the shaken passengers to get out of their seats.

Airline management later introduced the Aircraft Information Monitoring System (AIMS), an integrated software platform that controlled the aircraft's avionics and monitored pilots' flying techniques. This meant that, apart from starting and stopping the clock, none of the above was possible any more.

Nor was this a South African aberration. I once took a Delta Airlines 727 on a shuttle to New York after visiting my brother in Boston. Right after takeoff, I began to recognise signs of cowboy flying: high-speed flight, late descent, speed-brake usage and hard braking to make a quick turn off the runway – so hard that I felt the rare occurrence of the nose-wheel brakes kicking in. At the gate, the captain confirmed he was in a rush by being the first person off the plane. I felt right at home.

In general, successful co-pilots are like chameleons, adapting their flying styles to whichever captain they are flying with. You might operate conservatively on one trip and fly on the clackers the next. God help you if you get the captains mixed up. We also had to remember which captain had which quirk, such as the one who would reduce some of the cabin staff to tears by quizzing them on emergency procedures. (That guy was easy to identify: the cabin staff avoided him like the plague on and off the aircraft.)

Some, though, just had to be ignored. Once I was on a 747 doing

Cabin service for SAA passengers in 1980 (top) and 1978 (bottom)

a one-day shuttle between Portugal, Italy and Greece in the middle of one of our Lisbon trips when we entered a layer of ozone (O3). It was such a long, exhausting shuttle that we had a running joke about it. *Question: What has four legs and fucks aircrew? Answer: The Lisbon/Rome/Athens shuttle.* Because the distances between the cities were relatively short, we only needed a light fuel load on those sectors and would often cruise above 40 000 feet for maximum economy.

We quickly began to feel the effects of the ozone, a pungent and irritating natural gas found at very high altitude. Our eyes and throats itched, we had a burning need to cough and felt slightly short of breath. The Royal Family captain refused the co-pilot's request to descend out of the ozone layer.

'It's not going to harm you,' lectured the captain. 'It's just mind over matter.'

We stayed in the ozone layer.

The interphone dinged and the cabin crew chief asked, 'What's going on?' The passengers were complaining. With mule-like stubbornness, the captain repeated the mind-over-matter thing.

Five minutes later, the interphone dinged again. Two elderly passengers had passed out and three more were on oxygen. Could we please do something before someone dies?

The captain had gone to the bathroom (probably to cough and puke), so we immediately initiated a descent to a lower level.

He returned to his seat and never commented on the lower altitude or mentioned 'mind over matter' again. I think what he really meant was he didn't mind the ozone and no one else on the plane mattered.

Using the PA system was possibly the most stressful part of the job – especially as it had to be done in both official languages, English and Afrikaans.

Unlike some airlines, we flew leg for leg in SAA. That meant that the captain and co-pilot shared flying duties equally, normally alternating with each sector. And if you flew the sector, you spoke on the PA. Pilots screwed up this seemingly simple duty all the time. As there was no set PA format, you had to learn as you went along. Your PA technique got a little smoother over time but it never got easier.

One common PA mistake was to push the wrong selector button on the communications box, say VHF1 instead of PA. You would then entertain ATC and every aircraft on that channel with your poor PA technique until you released the transmit button – and after hearing everyone's caustic remarks you would have to do it all over again for your passengers.

Another mistake was to inadvertently press the PA hand-mike transmit button, awkwardly situated on a pedestal to the side of the pilot's leg, with the side of your shoe. You would then entertain your passengers with your cockpit chatter, some of which could be very salty, until the cabin staff came to tell you they didn't appreciate the way you were speaking about them.

In spite of it all, a small percentage of the pilots loved the sound of their own voices. They spent much of the flight yapping on the PA, even telling jokes or holding quizzes until everyone on board – especially me – wished they would just shut up and fly the jet.

And sometimes we would use the PA for information that was actually interesting.

A case in point: we were flying to Cape Town from the Northern Cape town of Upington, in the Orange River valley. The hot, dry climate here is ideal for growing grapes such as sultanas, and we always enjoyed seeing the beautiful green vineyard belt, which makes such a startling contrast to the desert scrub and yellow sand that lie just beyond the lush river valley.

But, this time, everything we expected to see was gone. In its place was a wide sheet of murky water with a few trees and grapevines peeping out of the muddy edges. Heavy rains in the Transvaal had overfilled the dams along the river, sending a dangerous flood surge downstream. The great length of the Orange had given the farmers a week to prepare, forcing them to pick their half-ripe grapes day and night, but it wasn't enough. We landed at Upington and told the sombre-looking ground staff about the widespread destruction. Half the harvest had been lost despite the early warning.

After we took off again, we decided we wanted to see what the floods had done to the Augrabies Falls, about 125 kilometres west of Upington. Diverting from a flight plan in order to do some sightseeing would be an instant firing offence today, but back then we simply advised ATC we'd be going there before proceeding on track to Cape Town. We turned 90 degrees right and followed the river at 5 000 feet altitude until we approached the falls. On the way, the captain advised the passengers where we were going and what they were going to see. One of the passengers was a hydrology professor who asked to come to the cockpit for a better view and offered to give a running commentary over the PA.

Instead of the usual-size falls, Augrabies – named for a Khoi word meaning 'the place of the great noise' – was a mass of roiling muddy water and mist that almost filled the valley more than 50 metres below. It was an awe-inspiring display of how violent nature can be. The professor calculated we were seeing four times the normal flow of the much larger Niagara Falls going over Augrabies, a staggering amount of fresh water heading for the Atlantic Ocean.

We circled the falls until the flight engineer got worried about our fuel. We'd spent a long time at low level and needed to set our heading for Cape Town. We landed 15 minutes late but gave those on board a once-in-a-lifetime experience. It's what we used to call good passenger service.

Needless to say, our passenger interactions weren't all fun.

In one especially sad incident, I was on a 747 flight to Madrid when an upset cabin crew chief came into the cockpit during the night to tell us that a woman in her eighties had died in economy class. The cabin crew had put out a call for any doctors on board and carried the passenger to first class, where there was more space to try and revive her. When it was clear that nothing could be done, the crew placed her in one of the translucent body bags we always had on board and moved her away from the shocked passengers.

Later, a cabin steward decided to move her distressed travel companions to the empty upper-deck seats (once used as a lounge).

We informed SAA on company radio and asked them to make arrangements for our arrival in Spain. An aircraft arriving in a foreign country with a dead body is automatically impounded until a judge confirms there has been no foul play. This can cause a long delay unless local authorities are already aware of the situation and have the appropriate officials waiting for the aircraft. We were assured that a Spanish doctor would meet our flight.

As the soft light of morning began to filter into the cockpit, I stepped back to the upper-deck cabin to see how the dead woman's companions were doing. I got a shock. They were dozing in the last row of seats, and as it grew lighter in the cabin, I could clearly see a pair of feet in a translucent body bag sticking into the aisle behind them.

The chief had brought the woman's body upstairs and placed it behind the seats to hide it – the same seats where the steward later placed her grieving companions.

I feared a disaster if they woke up and looked around, so I quietly draped a blanket over the jutting feet, then told the air hostess to wake them and tell them they needed to return to their original seats for landing.

After waiting 20 minutes on the Madrid apron, the doctor arrived to check the dead passenger. He was led to the upper deck and the bagged body was brought out from behind the seats. The doctor took a quick look and asked who had determined that the person was dead.

The chief held up his hand.

'And how long has she been sealed in this body bag?' he asked.

'About six hours,' replied the chief.

'Okay, she's dead now for sure,' he pronounced and cleared the passengers to disembark.

The last part of the story was even sadder. The woman had been due to remain on the plane for the next leg of the flight, to Frankfurt, but as she was deceased she was no longer considered a passenger. Instead, she was classed as freight for the next leg. We were told that her passenger ticket to Frankfurt was voided and her family would have to pay, by the kilogram, for her body and a coffin to travel in a cargo hold. I don't know exactly how it worked, but a part of me wished we could have kept her hidden behind the seats and only 'discovered' her on the last leg.

Chapter 15
Near Misses

I had barely completed a year on 727s when SAA stopped operating the type and sold them to another carrier. Typical of a state-run enterprise, they screwed up the sales contract so badly that the airline was required to refit the machines with modern avionics before delivery – the same equipment they'd refused to provide their own pilots with because of the high cost.

I made my last 727 landing on a Friday in Keetmanshoop, and started my 737 course the next Monday in Johannesburg. At least I got the weekend off.

Aside from taking roughly the same number of passengers, the Boeing 727 and 737 had few similarities. The basic 737 was a lightly built jet with two engines and two pilots. Nicknamed 'Fluff' (Fat Little Ugly Flying Fucker) or 'Fluffy' by its pilots, the 737 was a 727 with all the fun and performance removed. But it was an accurate example of how future airliners were going to look and fly.

Our flying instructors were ex-727 pilots. They advised us to pretend it was a nice aircraft and to not make jokes about it to other 737 pilots. And not to keep calling it a light twin. SAA later purchased an advanced 737 version that actually performed quite well.

In the mid-1980s, SAA decided to decentralise some 737 internal crews to Durban and Cape Town to reduce their hotel expenses in those cities and improve crew utilisation. I was one of the lucky pilots selected to live in Cape Town. By this time I was married to Arlene, whom I'd known since we performed in a school play at Herzlia. We'd lost touch while I was in the air force but reconnected during my early days at SAA. Both of us were delighted to be leaving Johannesburg to go back home.

We bought a beautiful old gabled home in the Cape Town suburb of Fresnaye that we were told had been built for a retired sea captain. It had a curved teak bay window to give the old salt an unobstructed view of his beloved ocean, and a large cellar for his equally beloved wine collection. Apparently, he had loved children and liquor with equal gusto and his happy spirit remained in the house. The German couple we bought it from had received a higher offer from someone else but decided to sell it to us anyway because they thought we seemed a nice young couple – and because they hoped we too would have children in the house. We were living there when Morgan was born.

SAA's 737 co-pilots were the hardest-working pilots in the airline. Because the 737 only had a two-person flight crew, the co-pilot did most of the flight engineering (systems management) duties, in addition to regular flying. We often flew five legs a day, which could leave you quite tired on the last few sectors. It was particularly exhausting if bad weather required full instrument approaches at a couple of destinations. That was when you had to be careful not to make mistakes, as tiredness made it much easier to screw up.

I had several close calls on the 737.

One time, we were headed into the sleepy Garden Route coastal city of George, located on a beautiful rolling plain halfway between Cape Town and Port Elizabeth. The airport was named – and upgraded – for apartheid president PW Botha, who had a home in nearby Wilderness. Looking inland, the plain ends at the tall Outeniqua Mountains, which divides it from the much drier Little Karoo. That inland valley ends in another line of mountains, the Swartberg range, roughly parallel to the Outeniquas. Beyond that lies the arid Great Karoo.

As we usually approached George from the coastal side, the mountains were not typically an issue. But sometimes we approached from the interior, which meant we had to cross both mountain ranges first. As the airport had no radar, in overcast conditions – known as instrument meteorological conditions (IMC) – we first flew over the airfield at high altitude before descending over the coastal plain.

On this flight we were headed into George with solid cloud cover below. We descended to a safe altitude and then flew level, waiting until we were over the airport. The distance measuring equipment (DME) showed 13 miles to the airport, very close in aviation terms, when the clouds suddenly parted and we saw that we were passing over a mountain range. Confident that we were already over the coastal plain, we asked to visually continue the descent instead of passing overhead at high altitude.

ATC agreed to our request. The clouds closed up again below but we started to descend anyway. However, something was niggling the captain. He decided to stop the descent slightly above the altitude of the tallest mountain until we saw the ground again.

As we flew level, I actually felt annoyed at his timidity.

Then at 4 DME, only four miles to the field, the clouds opened again. We were passing over a second set of mountains. They were very, very close.

Fooled by the close DME, without knowing the exact distance to the mountain ranges, we initially thought we were passing the Outeniquas, but we were wrong – we'd first spotted the Swartberge. Luckily the captain had more sense than I did. If we'd continued descending as I'd wanted to do, we'd have flown directly into the Outeniquas.

I learned a big lesson about assuming anything that day. I also lost another cat's life.

Near Misses

Another near disaster was at Upington, where the summertime heat waves would rise off the scorching ground to obscure anything at a distance.

We were taxiing out for a sector to Cape Town that I would be flying. The 737 was fairly light and only required reduced thrust for this takeoff, but for no particular reason the captain elected to use max thrust instead.

As we taxied out, the tower ordered a maintenance truck off the runway and then cleared us for takeoff. We lined up and looked down the runway. It looked clear but heat waves obscured it beyond a point.

During the takeoff roll, I noticed something strange in the hazy distance. One of the white centreline markings seemed wider than the others. As a non-flying pilot, the captain had his eyes in the cockpit watching engine and flight instruments.

As we accelerated, I noticed with horror that the wide marking now looked like a white vehicle parked in the centre of the runway.

'There's a bakkie on the runway!' was all I managed to say.

Moments later we reached our Vr (rotate speed, to lift our nose off the runway) and I pulled the jet into a high nose attitude. We passed over the small pick-up truck at 50 feet. The driver's door was wide open. I could see someone crouching in a ditch next to the runway, presumably the driver. I felt a surge of anger and wanted to return immediately and hit him. Instead, we simply reported the dangerous incident to the tower and proceeded to Cape Town.

Later we found out what had happened. An electrician had parked on the runway and got out to fix a runway edge light, about 25 metres away. He had a radio in his vehicle but no portable radio with him. That was how he missed the call when the tower told him to clear the runway.

Neither we nor the tower noticed the truck on the runway, probably because he'd parked his white bakkie exactly on a white centreline marking and because of the obscuring heat waves. When the electrician saw the 737 bearing down on him he had two choices – try to move the truck or hide in the ditch. He chose the ditch, a sensible if cowardly choice.

The airline initially tried to blame us for the incident but changed their minds after seeing how impossible it was to discern anything at a distance through the heat waves. Whoever was to blame, it was much too close for comfort; if the captain had not randomly decided to use max thrust, we would have slammed into the vehicle before getting airborne.

Then there was the time we became forgetful ... The 737 has fuel tanks in each wing and a centre tank in the fuselage. Occasionally, the quantities in the wing tanks might differ from each other for one reason or another, creating a lateral weight imbalance.

This isn't a big problem. To fix it, we'd switch off fuel pumps from the lower-quantity tank and cross-feed from the fuller one until they were even, then restore all fuel pumps again. The trouble is to remember to stop fuel balancing once you've started and to switch on all the pumps again. One captain would clip a red clothes peg to his control column as a visual reminder that he was balancing. Another would clip his necktie. Most of us just tried to remember.

But on a flight to Harare, Zimbabwe, we both got distracted (lazy) and forgot we were balancing until very late in the flight. By the time we remembered and started to balance in the other direction, we had already exceeded the maximum wing tank fuel imbalance for landing.

Now that we had something to worry about, we paid close attention to our fuel situation. We flew faster to burn up some extra fuel, descended late and used the speed brake all the way down. Finally, we dragged the aircraft on a long final approach with gear and flaps down and only ceased fuel balancing 500 feet above the ground. It was just enough. We landed a few pounds within the maximum allowable limit for imbalance. Not my best day at the office.

Things often go wrong in flying. From mechanical failures to emergencies to bad weather, pilots have to be ready for all sorts of emergencies. And that's where the professionals set themselves apart from the amateurs.

On one of my 737 flights, we were cleared for a visual approach to runway 29 in East London and were stabilised on final approach four miles from touchdown. We'd been advised a light aircraft was passing the field at 1 000 feet altitude but ATC had told the pilot to stay well clear of the approach area. I was flying the leg and neither I nor the captain had the small plane in sight.

Suddenly I did.

The Cessna was crossing our approach path a bare quarter mile ahead of our jet. The small, high-winged machine rapidly filled our windscreen, moving from right to left, its propeller a whirling disc.

My C-47 training then came in useful. I banked hard right and pushed the rudder almost to the stop to quicken the turn. The light aircraft flashed by to our left and after a few moments I reversed the manoeuvre and re-established on final approach. Amazingly, the tower saw nothing, as they were searching for the traffic to the east of the field. The controller was really upset when we told him what the light aircraft pilot had just done. The Cessna pilot, who was a farmer, denied ever seeing our 737, which at a quarter mile must have looked like it was about to hit him in the face. God knows where he was looking, because if it had been out the window he definitely would've seen us if we'd come crashing through it.

I've even had to deal with flying emergencies when I was a passenger. One year, Arlene and I were flying on a commuter airline from Margate to Durban after spending a few days at a beach resort on the Wild Coast. From Durban, we planned to get an SAA flight to Johannesburg.

The commuter flight was on a single-engine, propeller-driven Piper aircraft with six seats and limited baggage space. I was looking forward to seeing the view from a much lower altitude than when I regularly flew over it.

The pilot said that one of the passengers could sit in the vacant front seat next to him. I instantly jumped into the seat, visibly annoying another guy who also wanted it. Too bad. I didn't tell the Piper pilot – who was a few decades older than me – that I was an airline pilot. I didn't want him to feel pressured by thinking I was watching him.

I noted that the Piper had inboard and outboard fuel tanks in both wings. The outboards were full and the inboards had a quarter tank each.

The commuter pilot was a 'toucher'. He liked to touch each instrument or selector as he worked through the checklist. When he reached the fuel selector, he set it to feed from tanks that showed almost empty.

This surprised me, but as I didn't know the fuel system on this particular aircraft, I assumed it was in the correct position. He taxied out, took off and we turned north along the rugged coastline at 1 500 feet altitude. However, my enjoyment was marred by the fuel selector being on tanks that seemed to be getting even emptier.

Once again, the conscientious pilot scanned and touched his instruments, including the fuel selector. He seemed to be satisfied but I still couldn't relax.

We flew northwards. The engine kept turning, so I figured the inboard tanks might have been getting a gravity feed from the outboard tanks. But I stopped looking at the view and decided to watch the fuel pressure gauge instead. If there was fuel pressure, I reasoned, there must be fuel.

To my great relief, Durban airport appeared on the horizon. Soon we were downwind abeam the runway and I began to relax. The pilot turned left to begin his final approach. He ran down landing flaps and pushed the pitch lever fully forward to set the propeller for landing.

At that moment the fuel pressure dropped to zero and the engine lost power.

The pilot made no attempt to re-establish it. Instead, he pushed the throttle wide open and stared wide-eyed at the rapidly changing perspective of the runway as we dropped further and further below the correct approach angle. A highway full of cars was just below us.

We clearly were not going to make it to the runway. I'd had enough. I reached forward and turned the fuel selector on to the full tanks. The fuel pressure shot up and the windmilling engine instantly caught with a roar. The surge of full power dragged us across the grassy approach area. The Piper crossed the runway threshold and thumped down hard onto the tarmac, its engine still blaring at full power.

The pilot came to his senses and closed the throttle. He brought the plane to a halt and turned to me, white-faced. 'What happened?' he asked me – a passenger! I explained about the fuel selector and he immediately tried to blame the Margate refueler for his troubles.

I wasn't interested. I told him that I was an airline pilot and this should be his last flight. Once we parked, I got out without saying another word. The passengers emerged, including the guy who had wanted the front seat. They had no idea what had just happened and he gave me a final glare as he walked away. 'You're lucky to be alive,' I muttered to his retreating back.

Arlene had been in the row behind me for the flight. The plane had been too noisy for me to whisper to her while we were in the air, but she'd seen me lunge forward as we were coming in to land and could see that I was furious.

'What happened?' she asked. I explained. Then she told me that the grumbling passenger had tried to get her to convince me to give up the front seat. He'd complained throughout the flight that he flew the route regularly, that the seat next to the pilot was 'his' – and wouldn't she rather have her husband next to her than in the front?

Arlene is not someone easily talked into anything, so she had no problem saying no. She's never been afraid of flying, but she told me as we walked towards the terminal that that she'd felt uncharacteristically uncomfortable when we boarded the plane. 'I just remember looking over at you and thinking that I might actually have been nervous if you hadn't been sitting right by the controls,' she said. 'My husband,' she told the irate man, 'is sitting in the right seat.'

Not all close calls had a good ending. As a short-range 737 co-pilot, it was a treat to be rostered for an international flight once a month or so. I was in London on one of those flights when I got an urgent message to come to the co-pilot's hotel room. When I got there, the other crew members had already gathered. 'We lost one,' the co-pilot told me grimly.

I didn't understand. He explained that one of our 747s had disappeared shortly before landing at Mauritius. Each SAA aircraft had a name as well as a registration number; the plane that had gone down was the *Helderberg*, registration ZS-SAS, a 747-244B Combi. Unlike regular 747s, the Combi had a freight compartment on the main deck behind the passenger cabin.

The details of the tragedy took a while to emerge and spawned a host of conspiracy theories. What was undisputed was that on a flight from Taiwan to Mauritius, a fire had started in a cargo pallet on the *Helderberg*'s main deck. It could not be extinguished and the plane broke apart before crashing into the ocean on 28 November 1987, killing all 159 people on board. Many believe the fire was caused by illegal munitions – perhaps rocket fuel – that SAA might have been carrying as part of the efforts to circumvent international sanctions against Pretoria. Others have blamed lithium batteries for starting the blaze. A more recent theory has suggested that the fire could have been caused by a flammable type of wiring fitted throughout the *Helderberg*.

For us in London the details trickled in, but by nightfall we still didn't know the names of the dead crew members or any details about the cause of the fire. I must admit I felt some dread about flying home the next day. No one expressed any reluctance to get on board but fear was thick in the cockpit as we took off. The co-pilot, who was flying the sector, was over-controlling the jet with rough, jerky movements before we all eventually calmed down and the flight landed safely in Johannesburg.

Years later, the Truth and Reconciliation Commission would go on to investigate the various theories about the cause of the *Helderberg* crash. It was only able to conclude with certainty that many questions still remain unanswered.

Chapter 16

'Koos, Power Lines!'

We stared at the fuel gauge and willed it to start rising, but two things were clear. The tank was not being refilled and we could not reach Windhoek without the extra fuel. The question of whether we'd make it to Windhoek wasn't what I'd had in mind when I'd decided to buy my own light aircraft with another SAA pilot to enjoy the stunning beauty of the Cape Peninsula from above.

As a SAAF pilot, I'd flown with several private pilots in their small planes. One had been a dentist with a Mooney, a class of high-performance light aircraft that we called 'Doctor Killers'. Medical professionals could afford to buy them, we said, but their pilot skills were only sufficient to fly them to the scene of their own accidents. I stopped accompanying the dentist when I realised he didn't know what he was doing – something he later proved by ripping out a set of visual approach slope indicators, or VASI, at Cape Town International Airport.

Koos, another Cape Town co-pilot, had agreed to buy the plane with me. We wanted something smaller, cheaper and sexier than a Mooney and we planned to do some aerial photography on the side to help make it pay for itself.

Koos had tracked down a classic Piper J-3 Cub for sale in Mariental, a small town in what was then still South West Africa. It belonged to a doctor who owned several aircraft, including a Beechcraft Bonanza, another Doctor Killer. The doctor agreed to pick us up in Windhoek with his Doctor Killer and fly us to Mariental to view the Cub.

'Koos, Power Lines!'

We took a jump-seat ride on an SAA flight to Windhoek and, as promised, a Bonanza was waiting for us on the apron. Just over an hour later, with the sun setting behind the spindly ironwood trees, the doctor landed at Mariental's small airfield. As it was too dark to see the Cub properly, we retired to his home for a braai. We drank cold beer and warm wine while a farm labourer grilled fragrant lamb ribs and boerewors over glowing coals. There were no vegetables or salad. The conversation was in Afrikaans and Koos indiscreetly commented on the braai's unhealthy fat-to-meat ratio. The portly, red-faced doctor disagreed. 'Doesn't shorten your life at all,' he assured us, gulping down another fatty *ribbetjie*. We hoped he'd survive until morning or we might lose our Cub.

After a hearty breakfast – more meat – he took us to view the Cub in an old metal hangar at the airfield. It was a beautiful 1940s J-3, with traditional yellow fabric that was covered with fine brown dust. Clearly, it had not been flown in quite some time.

The doctor was reluctant to tell us the whole story, but we later worked it out for ourselves. He'd bought the Cub for recreational flying but found the taildragger too much of a handful and had swiped a tree on landing, damaging a wingtip. He'd flown an aviation mechanic to Mariental in his Bonanza to repair the damage but never worked up the courage to fly the Cub again. That had been more than a year ago. It hadn't been flown since and needed an annual service in Windhoek to be flown legally.

If we could fly it there, the doctor proposed, he'd pay for the service and we could decide on the way if we wanted to buy it. Neither of us had ever flown a J-3 Cub before, but we instantly agreed to take it to Windhoek. I noticed the tyres looked a little flat. Could he pump them up? Sorry, he didn't have a tyre pump. Perhaps he could he give us some Cub flying tips? No, he couldn't. We were on our own.

The 170-mile trip to Windhoek in the Cub should take about two and a half hours, the doctor informed us, barely faster than driving. He didn't have a map but we could easily follow the road north to the city.

The Cub was a very basic machine. There was no electric starter; the engine was started by manually swinging the propeller. There was a small fuel tank behind the engine with a float gauge and a larger supplementary wing tank to refill the smaller tank by gravity feed. The entire electrical system ran off a small motorcycle battery in a wooden box behind the pilots.

We climbed in and the puffing doctor swung and swung the propeller until the engine finally caught. I tried to taxi the Cub to the runway but it proved to be almost unsteerable, completely un-responsive to rudder inputs. I desperately tried to remember how we used to taxi Harvards, but nothing seemed to work. Later we found out that the tailwheel steering mechanism was broken.

Koos gave it a try. Eventually he got the Cub roughly aimed down the runway and we took off. We'd planned to try a couple of practice landings, but the first one went so badly that we set our heading for Windhoek rather than embarrass ourselves any further.

The flight in the little aircraft was exhilarating and we were enjoying ourselves immensely. As we flew northward, the fuel float gauge in front of the windscreen dropped lower and lower. When it was about an inch above the rim of the fuel cap, we opened the fuel valve to start refilling it from the wing tank. Nothing changed. The float continued to drop. We stared at the gauge and willed it to start rising, but it was clear the tank was not being refilled.

The float was bobbing on empty when we arrived over the tiny town of Rehoboth. Desperate to find somewhere to land, we spot-ted the rough outlines of an abandoned airstrip to the west of the town. Koos had been doing a better job of flying the Cub than me so he agreed to attempt a landing on the old strip. If he repeated the high bounce of our first landing, this would not go well.

We were both nervous as he lined up with the runway. We

passed over a power line on short finals and landed with a firm thump on the overgrown gravel strip. We passed some bushes, swept past a tree, then more bushes and a series of meerkat holes and finally ground to a halt in a cloud of dust, amazingly still in one piece.

We climbed out of the Cub in relief. Three men watched us from near a rusty yellow bulldozer parked some distance away. We walked over in the stinging heat. They were making their lunch, braaiing some thin wors over a small fire. They seemed curiously uninterested in us, considering we'd just landed next to their bulldozer, but they agreed to drive us to a telephone. I think their first concern had been that we'd landed to eat their wors.

We telephoned the doctor and calmly told him what had happened, expecting him to be really shocked. 'Yes,' he said as if we were having a conversation about fatty ribs. 'I also had some trouble with that, so I put on a new automobile fuel cap to fix it.' Well, it didn't fix it, you *doos*. And thanks for only telling us about it now.

We went back to the Cub, determined to abandon it there and hitch a ride to Windhoek. To our amazement, we noticed that the front tank was now full. In fact, fuel was leaking from the cap and running onto the ground. 'What the fuck?' Koos said. It became clear what the problem was. Negative pressure (a vacuum) over the wing fuel cap had inhibited the fuel transfer in flight. It could easily be fixed in Windhoek, but first we needed to get back into the air. The bulldozer/wors guys had decided to make our lives easier by scraping the bushes off the runway and were filling in the worst potholes in a billowing cloud of dust.

By now, residents who'd seen or heard our aircraft landing were arriving in droves at the old airfield to see what was going on. We were about to give them some good entertainment.

I sat in the cockpit and pushed the awkward heel brakes while Koos repeatedly swung the propeller until the engine caught. After he climbed in, we tested the magnetos (ignition) and found one of the two systems was now stone dead. That is normally grounds for shutting down and getting maintenance. But these were not normal times, and anyway, the maintenance was in Windhoek. To a cheer and waves from dozens of kids, Koos opened full power and the Cub started to roll down the freshly cleared strip.

The soft ground, underinflated tyres and faulty magneto now took their toll. We reached 40 mph (about 65 kph) and that was it. The Cub refused to reach its normal takeoff speed of 55–60 mph (88–100 kph). The end of the strip was approaching fast and the plane still wouldn't accelerate.

Then I remembered the power lines!

'Koos!' I yelled. 'We must fly!' No response.

'Koos! Power lines, we must fly *now*.'

He got the message and pulled back hard on the stick. Despite the dangerously low speed, the Cub came instantly unstuck and we whizzed over the power lines by mere inches. Then he dropped the nose to gain speed and we skimmed low over the bushes before starting a slow climb away from the ground. I looked back at Koos's white, sweating face and he stared at mine. Holy shit, that was close. This plane was determined to kill us. I now wanted to get rid of it as soon as possible.

The underpowered Cub inched higher until we were at most a couple of thousand feet above the ground, dropping in downdrafts and rising in thermals. It simply wouldn't climb any further. With a feeling of dread, I remembered that Windhoek was surrounded by mountains. There was no way we had enough altitude to clear them. We worried about it all the way to Windhoek but eventually we got through by following a pass between the peaks.

Now just one more obstacle remained – the landing. With a series of bounces, Koos touched down on the paved runway and coaxed the unresponsive J-3 to the maintenance hangars. We both literally fell out of the cockpit, emotionally drained. We stood side by side looking at the little yellow plane that had made nervous wrecks out of us. As we watched, one tyre went completely flat with a soft hiss.

'Should we buy it?' I asked Koos.

'Yeah, let's buy it.'

'Okay.'

We left the J-3 at the maintenance hangar with a firm promise from the works foreman that he'd personally attend to every item on the long list we gave him, as well as doing the annual inspection. He looked like the reliable sergeant major type from SAAF hangars, so we trusted him. A mistake.

The flight to Windhoek from Mariental in the J-3 was just a short hop, or at least was supposed to have been. Flying from Windhoek to Cape Town would be a two-day marathon that needed careful planning. The navigation would be fairly simple. In the main, we'd follow the major roads southward. But first and most important, I needed to learn how to fly a Cub properly.

The SAA training captain who'd checked me out on a Beechcraft Baron for my senior commercial licence was also a renowned expert on Cubs. In fact, he had an amazing low-level Cub routine that he regularly performed at airshows. (A year later, he used our machine in such a performance at Stellenbosch airfield.) He readily agreed to give me an hour's training on his own J-3.

We met at Grand Central Airport, a popular airfield for light aircraft training, located midway between Johannesburg and Pretoria. The captain swung the propeller, and the J-3 started instantly. He climbed into the back seat and told me to taxi out. I expected the same steering awkwardness with his Cub, but to my surprise, it was easy to control. I realised our machine had a steering problem in addition to its other issues.

We had a great hour's flying, finishing with circuits and landings at Grand Central. The captain was such an amazing pilot that he demonstrated a touch and go on a tiny strip for radio-controlled aircraft. He showed me it was better to approach high and then sideslip to ensure a pinpoint landing, along with other special techniques applicable to an underpowered aircraft with a large wing area. It was invaluable information; Koos and I had been trying to fly the Cub like a Boeing 737. The captain refused payment for the lesson, asking me instead to make a donation to charity. A real *mensch*, as well as a great pilot.

A month later we were back at the Windhoek maintenance hangar. Our plan was to inspect the aircraft and prepare it for a dawn departure to Mariental, where we'd pay the doctor and collect the J-3's logbooks. Then we'd continue south to a tiny strip that Koos knew from his SAAF days flying an Albatross. We'd refuel and stay overnight at a small motel close to the strip, then get airborne at dawn for the very long, non-stop leg to Cape Town. We expected fine weather the whole way and light winds in Cape Town. This was important, as the fabric-covered Cub is a lightweight machine and the wind can really howl in Cape Town. (Later, when we became very confident with our J-3, we'd operate in wind up to 25 knots.)

We got a shock when we walked into the hangar in Windhoek. The Cub was standing in a far corner and we could see that the tyre was still flat! We could even see the illegal automobile fuel cap. The mechanics clearly hadn't touched it at all. We cornered the foreman in his office and asked him how the annual service had gone. 'Fine,' he beamed, 'no problems, all done.'

Then we let him have it, finishing with a threat to have his maintenance licence revoked. 'Give me this afternoon,' he pleaded. 'I'll get my best man on it and have everything done by tonight.' We were furious. He'd been quite prepared to let us fly a faulty aircraft over inhospitable terrain to save his own skin. We warned him that if we found a single loose screw in the morning, his licence wouldn't be worth five cents.

As the sun peeped over the horizon, I lifted the Cub off the runway and started a gentle, climbing turn to gain altitude. It felt like a different machine after the previous day's frantic repairs and servicing. My training now made flying the Cub a pleasure instead of an anxious affair. Within 15 minutes, we were well clear of the mountains and set course to the south. We wouldn't be back, but it turned out we weren't yet done with the scumbag foreman and his second-rate work.

We waved to our new bulldozer/wors friends as we passed over Rehoboth. The newly scraped strip still didn't look inviting.

At Mariental, I positioned the Cub on a high final approach, exactly as demonstrated by the captain who'd taught me. Koos immediately got excited. 'Get down, get down, you're too high.'

'Relax, Koos,' I yelled. 'You're in a Cub but still thinking like a 737 pilot.' I closed the throttle and sideslipped to a smooth touchdown right on the markers. Koos was impressed. 'Nicely done, you actually learned something.' I smiled. That was as complimentary as Koos ever got. We paid the doctor (who actually looked a little fatter), collected all the Cub's documents and proudly took off in our own aircraft. We did a low-level wing waggle past the hangar and set off southward, this time for good.

The flight to our overnight fuel stop was uneventful. The gravity transfer from the wing tank initially refused to feed again, so we slowed almost to a stall to break the vacuum. Once the fuel began to flow, we resumed normal cruise. We'd learned that lesson well and neither of us wanted to repeat our Rehoboth experience.

The airfield had a single runway, just above the mountainous belt that lies north of the Orange River, the border with South Africa. We refuelled and pushed the Cub into an empty hangar for the night. After dinner, we sipped miniature bottles of whisky from the SAA flight and Koos told me a hilarious story from his air force days.

Shortly after he'd joined 27 Squadron in Cape Town as a new co-pilot, he was assigned to an eight-hour patrol mission with a CF commander. The squadron's primary task was coastal patrol, using the twin-engine, propeller-driven Albatross – the Italian-made Piaggio P.166 – whose main claim to fame was that it efficiently converted fuel into noise.

Before strapping himself in, the grizzled CF commander put a long, slim metal cylinder into the back of the Albatross. Koos was too junior to ask him about it so just got on with the job. Soon they were flying on their patrol route 20 miles off the west coast, heading north. Koos was required to give a progress and position report once an hour to the air force radio station on HF (high frequency, long-range radio). They were patrolling off the rugged Namaqualand coastline when the CF commander suddenly turned the Albatross towards the land. Once over the coastline, he put down the landing gear and flaps and made an approach onto a barely visible strip cut into the coastal scrub.

Koos didn't know what the hell was going on. The only thing he could think of was that the old guy had suddenly gone crazy. They touched down and slowed to taxi speed, but instead of stopping, the commander taxied the Albatross off the end of the strip and down a rough cutting that led to the sea. Koos said his eyes were wide like saucers as they bounced down the narrow, potholed path. He figured that even if he survived this nightmare, his flying career would be over before it started.

The path ended at a wide turnaround circle next to the beach. The CF guy made a U-turn in a cloud of dust and cut both engines. He then reached into the back, grabbed the long metal cylinder and twisted off the end. He pulled out a segmented rod and said his first words to Koos since turning towards the coast. 'I'm going fishing, *boet.*'

And for the next three hours he did, along with slugging down a couple of beers he'd stashed in his flight bag. Every hour, Koos dutifully returned to the plane, switched on the radio and made a position report as if they were still out patrolling the ocean. Without radar coverage, no one knew otherwise. Koos said he returned from his first mission a wiser and more cynical pilot. He had been taught that flying and drinking don't go together. He'd just learned that flying, drinking and fishing did.

At sunrise the next day our little yellow plane sped down the runway and into the air. We turned right to follow the road that cut through the increasingly rugged terrain, and kept climbing as the valley deepened and mountains began to loom on both sides. We were about 2 000 feet above the valley floor when all hell broke loose. It started with a mild shaking and suddenly the turbulence slammed into the little plane. I looked at the wings, amazed they were still attached. Bam! It hit us again and we started descending fast!

It wasn't my first encounter with clear air turbulence. On one of my 737 flights I'd been coming into Durban for the final approach of a five-sector trip. It had been a beautiful, clear and calm night. Everything felt normal until three miles from touchdown. Suddenly it felt like a giant hand was pushing the jet upwards and the speed started to increase rapidly.

I'd pulled off some thrust and pushed the nose down to try and stay on the landing path (the electronic three-degree slope to the runway), but it was useless. I realised we were in the hands of a powerful type of microburst, or thermal, despite there not being a cloud in sight. I didn't want to wait for the downdraft side before giving up the approach, so I executed a precautionary go-around while the captain told the tower what had happened. No earlier flights had reported any turbulence, so we hung around for a few minutes to allow the rough air to move away before positioning for another attempt.

The 737 had enough fuel for one more landing attempt before we'd have to proceed to Bloemfontein, our alternate airport. At four miles the plane began to shake. It felt like we were on a cobbled road but the speed remained fairly stable. And then suddenly we were through the disturbance, the air smoothed

Arlene and I in the Piper Cub

A Cub's-eye view of Cape Town's Clifton Beach

down like nothing had happened, and I landed normally.

That turbulent event had been weird but not dangerous. What was happening to us in our Piper Cub was dangerous.

'Koos, we've got to get out of this,' I yelled. He'd already opened full power but our engine was like gnats' wings in a windstorm. It made absolutely no difference to our rapid descent. At this sink rate we'd strike the ground within a minute and there was nothing we could do about it.

At that moment, we entered a different part of the mountain wave – the turbulence caused when high ground disturbs the horizontal air flow – and, just as suddenly as we'd started descending, we started to climb. I mean really climb, at ten times the best climb rate I'd ever seen in the Cub. When we were at a safe altitude, Koos throttled back below cruise power. We just kept going up. The wave spat us out at 8 000 feet above the valley floor. It was one of the scariest experiences I'd ever had in an aircraft.

We took time to assess the damage. There was a sulphuric smell in the cockpit. Koos found that the motorcycle battery had jumped out of its housing and was lying upside down in the wooden box. Battery acid had spilled all over the logbooks, which were soaked with the stuff. By the time we got to Cape Town, the pages had started to disintegrate. The acid also ruined most of our luggage, but that was the least of our worries. If the battery was dead, our radio wouldn't work, and we couldn't enter Cape Town airspace without one. Luckily, there was just enough juice left to keep it going until touchdown.

The rest of the long leg was uneventful. Seven hours after we took off, the Cub touched down sweetly at its new home, almost drained of fuel. We climbed wearily out of the cramped cockpit and decided to send it straight to the maintenance hangar for a checkout. It was just as well we did.

My phone rang a few days later. The maintenance manager asked us to come in; there was something he wanted to show us.

A few hours later, I was looking at the Cub's engine with the streamlined cowls removed. 'We found signs of leakage around the inlet manifold,' he explained, 'so we removed it to see if one of the gaskets was cracked. Let me show you what we found.' He opened his hand and showed me four greasy inlet gaskets. 'Every one of these is the wrong size. They're too big, not made for your engine. I'm amazed you didn't overheat and seize the engine or burn your valves. In addition, the propeller was out of balance and not properly set. Each blade was at a different angle.' The list of problems went on and on, including the broken steering mechanism. Remember, this was after a major service!

I began to realise we were lucky to have made it at all.

A week later I flew the Cub again. It was a different aircraft that cruised 25 per cent faster, was easy to taxi and started with the first swing of the prop every time. Our ugly duckling had bitten us a few times, but it finally evolved into a beautiful, tame swan.

Chapter 17
Jumbo Co-Pilot

Flying a jumbo jet is like driving a double-decker bus from the top deck. When you sit in a Boeing 747 perched 30 feet (9 metres) above the ground, your normal visual references don't work so well. Taxi speed is difficult to assess because you're always moving much faster than you realise, so we would use electronic groundspeed readouts instead of just eyeballing it. For landing height we relied on our flight engineer's chants of '100, 50, 30, 20, 10' from the radio altimeter showing our exact height as we neared the ground. (These callouts became automated on newer altimeters.)

I learned all of this when my SAA seniority number came up again at the end of the 1980s. I was a little reluctant to move on to the 747. I enjoyed the intensity of internal flying with up to five takeoffs and landings a day, sometimes for three days in a row. And I chafed with impatience on the longer sectors. In flying terms, I had a short-range backside.

Then there was the fact that we lived in Cape Town and most international flights left from Johannesburg. It was possible to live in the Cape and do the two-hour commute to Johannesburg for a long-range flight, but it made every overseas trip half a day longer and you were always at someone's mercy for a jump seat.

Still, it was a bad idea to refuse promotion. While many captains refused 747 command in order to stay on the internal fleet, it was risky – perhaps career-ending – for a co-pilot to do the same. And that was how I found myself back in ground school.

This being my third SAA course made some things much easier.

For example, I knew how to sleep with my eyes open during the excruciatingly boring Boeing technical slide presentations.

I was easily the worst lander in my training group. I found gauging the Boeing 747 landing flare very difficult after the much smaller 737. In flying jargon, I had no idea where the ground was. In consequence, I would either slam into the ground or float down the runway.

Mistakes like that could leave me feeling down. During one of those low points my younger cousin Tony suggested we go out to eat with some of his SAAF friends. Tony had followed in my footsteps by becoming a SAAF pilot and then moving into the commercial flying world. He still claims he had to leave the air force because our shared surname meant he was constantly being blamed for my misdeeds. I'd been staying with him at his Pretoria flat during my training as he was always good company and I could catch a train directly to the SAA training centre.

Tony loved practical jokes and had a particular fascination for false teeth. He had walking teeth, chattering teeth and a set of genuine false uppers that he usually kept in his pocket. They came along to our dinner that night at a popular local steakhouse, which had an extensive, help-yourself, mayo-heavy salad bar preferred by the meat-and-potato-loving clientele.

'Watch this,' said Tony while we sat drinking beer at our table. He went to the salad bar and pretended to fill his bowl. Then he took the false teeth from his pocket and pushed the set into the potato salad, casually covering it with a few big pieces. He then sat down, very pleased with himself. Within moments, a customer took a large spoonful of potato salad. I saw the choppers lift out of the bowl, only to drop off her spoon at the last minute. I was starting to feel better already.

The grinning teeth were now coated in lumpy potato salad, in-distinguishable from the rest of the bowl. To our unending mirth, one of his SAAF friends came back to our table with the toothy

Jumbo Co-Pilot

Morgan's first cockpit visit

SAA Boeing 747-200 ZS-SAN 'Lebombo' in the 1970s

prize on his plate. We watched his look of confusion turn to horror as he recognised what he was trying to eat.

He realised what was going on when he saw Tony and I almost catatonic with laughter at the other end of the table. In true SAAF style, he not only finished his salad but also licked the teeth clean.

Back on the course, my landing issues continued until I received a casual tip from a seasoned co-pilot. The jumbo's flare – when you raise the aircraft's nose to soften touchdown – normally starts at 30 feet AGL. He advised me to ease back ever so slightly on the control column at 50 feet to break the rate of descent, and then start the usual flare at 30 feet. That minute adjustment, along with a 727-style 'roll on' technique, ended my battle and made landing the big jet a pleasure. Not that I didn't slam it in now and again, but at least I always knew where or why my landing went wrong.

Once I finally got on the line, I routinely bid for international flights that originated from Cape Town so I didn't have to commute to Johannesburg.

One of those was a seven-day trip to Rio de Janeiro. This sprawling city, with its two airports, is situated on a beautiful coastal plain surrounded by steep mountains. Despite its visual appeal, in summertime the picturesque geography constantly generates thunderstorms. The bad weather, combined with the ring of mountains, makes Rio one of the most dangerous approaches in the world. Because of this, the Brazilian authorities developed unique procedures. If you didn't hear from the air traffic controller for 30 seconds once you'd begun the approach procedure, you were required to execute an immediate go-around. The same immediate go-around held for crossing certain radials (bearings) from a beacon.

Descending into Rio was a tense procedure. Because of the heavy cloud cover, you often didn't see the mountains; you just knew they were there. Usually, the first time you saw the ground was when you popped out of the clouds with the runway straight ahead. Except for one time when there wasn't a cloud in sight and we did the approach procedure in perfect visibility.

Frankly, it scared the crap out of me.

Following the procedure exactly, we flew directly towards a mountain and turned away shockingly close to it towards another mountain before finally swinging towards the safety of the runway on the flat plain. Visual approaches are generally desirable, but in Rio give me the cloud-covered approach every time. I knew what the mountains looked like; I just didn't like seeing them that close up.

Other destinations had their landing challenges too.

Mauritius, for example, had two quirks to consider when landing towards the east. First, the runway wasn't long enough to float down looking for a soft touchdown. The jumbo was a heavy aircraft and you had to get your stopping effort started as soon as possible. Second, there was a hump smack in the middle of the touchdown zone, which left you with three choices: land before the hump, land on it – always a hard landing – or try to land beyond it, which meant floating down.

I was more than a little nervous when we had to return one night for a maximum-weight landing. We'd departed Mauritius for Taiwan and were already in the cruise when we realised that the radar, which had tested out fine on the ground, was no longer working. Even when we switched systems, it stubbornly refused to show any radar returns on the screen. The route northward was always choked with thunderstorms, especially around the ITCZ (the inter-tropical convergence zone around the equatorial belt), so there was no question of continuing on to Taiwan without it.

We got ATC clearance to turn around and began to dump fuel down to landing weight.

The 747 can take off much heavier than it can land. Normally, fuel is burned up during the flight, but if you return quickly it's necessary to dump excess fuel overboard. The dumped fuel vaporises almost instantly into the atmosphere. I turned in my seat to look at the wingtip, where the fuel jettison nozzles were situated. Even though it was dark, I could see a thick, silvery stream of fuel pouring into the airstream. We were now fully committed to going back to Mauritius.

Although I was flying the sector to Taiwan, I wondered if the captain was going to let a newish co-pilot attempt a max-weight landing on a short runway. That question was answered when he turned to me and asked straight out, 'Rob, can you do it?' Despite my doubts, I didn't hesitate. 'Yes.'

It was settled. I'd do the landing.

There were four unusual factors at play with this night landing. A normal approach speed at the end of a long sector was about 130 knots. We'd be landing tonight at 160 knots. In addition, the 747 was about 100 000 pounds (45 000 kilograms) heavier than normal, which would make it tougher to stop on the short runway.

We'd be departing again as soon as possible. If I overheated the brakes – very easy to do on a heavy landing – it would delay our departure. Plus there was the hump in the touchdown zone, which made the first three factors even trickier.

There was so much to worry about that I decided not to think about it at all. I was an experienced pilot expected to cope with difficult situations. I would just do my job to the best of my ability, and if that wasn't good enough, I shouldn't be flying a 747.

It went very well. I landed beautifully just ahead of the hump and decelerated with plenty of runway to spare. The brake temperatures peaked in amber mid-range – not an issue at all. The captain was pleased, I was pleased and we departed Mauritius 45 minutes later.

It was a taste of things to come. When I began flying Boeing 747 freighters for a Japanese company a few years later, almost every landing would be a max-weight landing.

Meanwhile, a new rule was about to change our overseas lives. Until 1990, only married crew members could get free or heavily discounted fares for their spouses. Cabin crew had long demanded the same companion rights for their partners. Now crew could get anyone – friends as well as family – on a flight for a ten per cent fare, provided they travelled on standby.

As a boy pilot, I'd spent countless days killing time or just wandering around aimlessly on long layovers. Smartphones and music-streaming services had yet to be invented, so I'd made up a portable music centre, consisting of a CD player, a pair of quality powered speakers and international power adapters, that fitted into a camera bag. It meant dragging an extra bag around, but the ability to listen to my favourite music made my hotel room feel pleasant instead of as if I was in a little prison cell.

Now that I was a co-pilot, I decided that I wanted to use my time overseas more constructively, or at least to have more fun. The offer of companion tickets for friends would help make this happen.

One of my first 'companions' was Andrew, a good friend from Cape Town. He was a food fundi, a painter and an architect. He was also a photographer and often flew in the Cub until he grew tired of being airsick.

Andrew joined me on a week-long trip to Lisbon. He sat enthralled in the cockpit jump seat as I manoeuvred the 747 under radar control towards the city's runway in the predawn darkness.

'Can you see the runway?' the captain asked me. He wanted to transition to a visual approach to shave a few moments off the flight time. This is a standard question to the flying pilot. I glanced up from the flight instruments, but the runway lighting was still lost in a sea of city lights.

'Not yet,' I answered.

'Can you see the runway now?' he asked a few moments later. Same problem, and I wasn't going to be pushed into committing to a visual without having the runway in sight. 'No, not yet.'

Anxious Andrew's voice from the jump seat: 'How are you going to land if you can't see the runway?'

Hilarity all round the flight deck.

Overall, the 747 was an easy machine to fly, with few vices. However, its sheer size and weight caused some flight effects that could catch an unwary pilot.

Because of its weight, 830 000 pounds (378 000 kilograms) on takeoff, the 747 has much more momentum than any other airliner. It'll mush through the air for a while before doing what you want it to do. For example, to level a 737 in the climb, you start levelling off 50 feet before your required altitude. In the 747, you need a 200-feet lead.

Descent is even worse. You need to start slowing your rate of descent 1 000 feet before your required altitude or you'll blow right through it. I saw a new captain do just that in a 747SP in Europe. He was using the speed brake for an ATC-expedited descent and, because he had left it too late, only managed to level 800 feet below the required altitude. The Swiss ATC controller went crazy when we bust through our assigned altitude.

The same applies to speed control. Once the airspeed sets up a decaying trend, especially with landing gear and flaps down, it takes a positive effort and lots of power to stop or reverse it.

On one flight during my boy pilot days, a Royal Family captain terrified us by responding ineffectively to his decaying airspeed on final approach. We ended up 20 knots below bug speed (minimum approach speed), very close to the stall warning. He needed almost full power to reverse the trend.

Another effect of the 747's size is oversteering while taxiing. Because the pilot sits such a long way forward of the main wheels, and even slightly in front of the nose wheel, it's necessary for the cockpit to go well past the centreline during turns, sometimes almost to the edge of the taxiway in order to keep the main wheels on the centreline. To assist in rapid turning, the inner main gear turns in the opposite direction to the nose wheel. It takes some practice to get it right but, despite its size, the jumbo can use any standard taxiway or turnoff at an airport.

A thrilling/scary view from the flight deck is a 747 approaching to land in a strong crosswind. It's not a performance or safety problem, it's a perception problem: the long distance from the main wheels to the pilot means the nose can point well off the centreline of the runway. At normal approach speeds, the jumbo's nose is pointed 12 degrees to the left or right of the runway in a maximum crosswind. That means on short finals, the pilot is almost looking down the runway edge lights to keep the main wheels on the centreline. Only in the flare is the nose brought back to the centreline while maintaining runway direction with cross-controlling. Some airlines simply land with the drift angle (heading offset) still on.

Either way, it's an eye-opening sight.

PART 3

THE JAPAN YEARS

Chapter 18
Kabuki Flying

International economic sanctions had all sorts of unexpected effects on South Africa in the 1980s. At state-owned South African Airways, the financial boycotts to protest apartheid bit deep into the airline's route structure. Some countries refused to let us land; African countries denied us overflight rights. The result was that by the late 1980s, there were too many pilots for the shrinking number of flights. SAA's response was to second some of its pilots, allowing us to operate flights for foreign carriers.

Among these was a Japanese freight airline that wanted a number of SAA pilots for a four-year contract. Unusually, they insisted on selecting the pilots themselves. Until then, SAA had simply allocated us according to our places on the seniority list.

The carrier, Nippon Cargo Airlines (NCA), wanted us to operate Boeing 747Fs (freighters) from John F Kennedy International Airport (JFK) in New York to Narita in Japan via Anchorage, Alaska. Pilots could commute to the United States from anywhere in the world for their flights.

I was one of 40 who applied. Right away we found Japanese standards were much more stringent than what we were used to. We were sent to various locations in Johannesburg for exhaustive medical testing, including some eye tests we'd never been required to do before. Just 20 pilots advanced to the simulator and interview stage. Remember, the 20 who failed were all active and qualified SAA pilots!

Two smiling Japanese captains observed our simulator exercises.

We quickly learned that the smiles did not mean they were happy, or even satisfied – a valuable lesson for later. Those same pilots conducted the technical part of my interview. It did not go well.

'Schapiro-san, what are the maximum takeoff and landing weights of the 747?'

'I don't know.' They looked surprised and tried again.

'Schapiro-san, what are the engine temperature limits of the 747?'

'I don't know.'

'Really?' Now they looked shocked.

The problem was those questions were not answerable in SAA as we operated seven different 747 configurations, each with its own limits. To avoid confusion, we avoided memorising numbers and instead reviewed the limits from a checklist in the cockpit before departure.

I explained this. They nodded and asked me another question instead.

'Which factors limit the 747's maximum takeoff weight?'

I only remembered one out of seven possible factors. I left the interview depressed with my weak performance. The other candidates must have been even worse, though, because I was offered the job, along with three other co-pilots and four captains.

I went to Tokyo for the NCA training course that would get me my flying licence from the Japan Civil Aviation Bureau (JCAB). This was in early 1994, during the run-up to South Africa's first democratic election. I watched from afar as Nelson Mandela was inaugurated as the country's first black president.

In Tokyo I learned that there are two kinds of international pilots: those who have endured a JCAB course and the lucky ones who have not.

Typically, SAA pilots on foreign contracts had flown with other SAA pilots using SAA procedures. In fact, we'd often have a good laugh at hearing radio calls from aircraft operated by Luxair and

Air Mauritius, two of the early users of SAA cockpit crew. These two charter-type airlines operated SAA-owned 747SPs, a lighter, longer-range version of the traditional 747, painted in their own livery. Re-educating the SAA pilots turned out to be harder than repainting. Each airline has its own distinctive call sign, with British Airways' 'Speedbird' probably being the best known. SAA's call was 'Springbok'. The two client airlines simply used 'Luxair' and 'Mauritius'. This sometimes confused the leased pilots, and it became common and quite funny to hear 'Spring-luxair' or 'Springmauritius' call signs on the radio as SAA pilots battled unsuccessfully to forget their old moniker.

For NCA, we'd be flying with American, Canadian, British, Irish, Icelandic, Pakistani, Cypriot and, of course, Japanese pilots. We'd all been hired for our Western flying skills and our proficiency in English, the language of air traffic control around the world. This was especially important in high-traffic airports such as Chicago's O'Hare International, where there was no time to misunderstand radio communications.

The main difference between us was that Japanese pilots tended to fly exactly how they'd been taught in training: a one-size-fits-all approach to every situation. Western pilots had a more fluid attitude and often adapted procedures if the circumstances allowed them to do so safely.

Now we had to forget our past training and learn to fly the 747 in the somewhat old-fashioned Japanese manner – and do so convincingly enough to pass an oral and simulator check by JCAB examiners who spoke little English. In effect, the checkout would be a kabuki play and the cockpit a stage, with each movement, word or action pre-scripted. You didn't have to like it or even believe it was a good way to fly. You just had to perform your role, keeping your views hidden behind an unemotional façade.

On the upside, the airline didn't cut corners where it mattered. NCA's 747 freighters were magnificent compared to what

I was used to flying in SAA. Just a few years old, they were perfectly maintained and trimmed by All Nippon Airways (ANA) technicians, making them a pleasure to fly. The Japanese carrier did not tolerate defects, attending immediately to non-essential maintenance that could be legally deferred for weeks or even months. If an aircraft arrived in Tokyo with a known problem, a team of mechanics would be waiting on the tarmac to return it to technical perfection before the next flight.

One example of that perfection was supposed to eliminate something we used to call the 'finger game'.

The Boeing 747 is a four-engine jet, each engine controlled by a thrust lever, numbered 1 to 4, on the centre console. Each thrust lever is connected to its engine by a steel cable, much like the accelerator pedals in cars are connected to the engine throttle.

However, unlike a car, a 747 has four independent engines, which means that making them deliver exactly the same thrust when all four thrust levers are lined up needs skilled trimming of the steel cables by ground technicians. In SAA, the thrust levers had been all over the place. To maintain equal thrust in cruise, there was often more than an inch of throttle stagger between the four thrust levers. On approach, pilots would play the finger game by first setting all thrust levers evenly and then pushing one forward or pulling another back to try and get equal thrust across the board, a serious distraction at a critical time.

I thought this was a normal state of affairs on 747s until I joined NCA. To my amazement, all four thrust levers consistently delivered equal thrust, in cruise or on approach. I guess their technicians were more skilled or just tried a little harder. Either way, it was part of what made their 747s such a joy to operate.

They didn't get rid of the finger game completely, though. I soon discovered a variation that I'd never seen in SAA. While taxiing, some pilots would open or close thrust levers in a complex but completely unnecessary pattern. Sometimes they opened the two centre engines or, when turning, both on the left or the right or just the far left or far right engines.

The Boeing manual recommends equal thrust on all engines while taxiing, which works very well. So why did the pilots do it? Just a bad habit from their old airlines, I'm afraid. The foreign pilots in NCA came from myriad different outfits and brought some bad flying habits with them. By retraining everyone in the ANA training centre, NCA smoothed out the biggest differences between us. But some little quirks would always remain.

On our first jet-lagged day at the Tokyo training centre we had to transfer our Western flight hours to a Japanese logbook. The rules of what went where were so complex that it took more than an entire day.

Then we had to pass three general subjects: lights and signals, air law and radio. Answers had to be written out precisely like the model answer, often a long list of obscure items. We quickly suspected that the JCAB examiners weren't actually reading the papers but were looking for key words or phrases or simply the correct-length answer. Once, when we compared answers after the tough air law exam, we realised that half of us should have failed for misinterpreting a major question. However, we all passed – probably because the incorrect answer was the same length as our misguided ones.

The radio licence lectures were even stranger. Two senior Japanese observers sat in our class doing precisely nothing the entire week except glare at us. They had placed two thick textbooks on each of our desks that were completely indecipherable to a class that couldn't read Japanese. Our pleasant English-speaking lecturer explained they were required to be there by law.

Once the legally required subjects were out of the way, we began the mind-numbing routine of 747 technical school. We had to wear business clothes, which for me – who believed in only wearing sweatpants or shorts when I wasn't in uniform – meant

Secrets from the Cockpit

I had to have a jacket made by a tailor before I left Cape Town. I called it Hans because I thought the checked fabric pattern looked vaguely German.

Saving laundry costs by washing my clothes in my Tokyo hotel room

Lectures began at precisely 8.30 am with mutual silent bows to the instructor. At 11.30 we'd stop for lunch. Food at the efficiently run company cafeteria was always a tasty and reasonably priced choice of Western-style food or typical Japanese dishes. In general, we preferred the Japanese options. After making our selections, we *gaijin* (foreigners) sat together at one of the long lunch tables, ignored by airline staff and employees busy with their own lunches. Or so we thought.

I found out later that many were secretly watching us, deeply amused by our strange eating habits. Our chief crimes were drizzling soy sauce over our rice instead of putting it in a little bowl for dipping, and awkwardly using chopsticks to raise food to our mouths instead of raising the whole bowl. We in turn could not get used to the noisy Japanese practice of loudly slurping noodles from the bowl into the mouth.

I also learned later that my jacket wasn't the only thing with a nickname. My Japanese colleagues in the training centre started calling me 'Super Mario' because my wavy dark hair and moustache reminded them of the popular digital game character, causing much hilarity on the administration floor. Luckily, I'm always happy to amuse, especially with my face.

Adding to the stress of our training course was our separation from our families. No matter how upmarket the hotel, we were away from our wives and children, unable to cook our own meals and having to grapple with complex training aggravated by cultural misunderstandings.

NCA presumably recognised this, and included in our contracts paid tickets and accommodation for a two-week visit from immediate family. Arlene was able to fly out for a visit during my first training course, but I was so busy with ground school that I could barely spend any time with her during the day. Luckily, she was happy to explore Tokyo on her own, claiming – probably correctly – that she'd seen more of the city in three days than I had in three months.

Morgan was a toddler at the time of her first visit, so she'd left him in Cape Town with his doting grandparents. By the time I went on my second course, we had moved to the US. This time, five-year-old Morgan came with her from Boston.

One Sunday morning, I rushed downstairs to meet the airport bus and immediately saw Morgan's little face pressed against the window. I was relieved when he pointed and smiled at me – two months is a long absence for a child. His smile grew wider when he realised that he had his own luxury hotel room, complete with minibar (which we'd emptied). He was also enchanted by the tiered fountain in the centre of the hotel lobby, jumping with excitement as he watched the water rise and fall.

We went to one of my regular small yakitori restaurants for our first Tokyo meal together. Morgan, always a picky eater, was badly jet-lagged and definitely not willing to try anything new. Arlene pulled a small box of breakfast cereal from her bag to placate him. One of the staff brought him a bowl. Morgan looked at the dry Cheerios and decided they needed something more. He picked up the can of lemonade we'd ordered for him and carefully poured it onto the cereal. The customers and the restaurant owner gasped in horror. Arlene was too jet-lagged to care. I knew I might never be able to show my face in that restaurant again.

Morgan adamantly clung to American food for the rest of that trip. We had to buy a jar of Skippy peanut butter and some awful white bread at an outrageous price from a supermarket that specialised in imported foods and take these supplies with us every time we went out for a meal. Arlene and I would order our own food, then haul out the Skippy to make Morgan a sandwich. Other diners would avert their eyes to spare our shame.

Of course, Morgan did eventually develop an appreciation for Japanese cuisine – especially sashimi. When he visited me on a later course, as a teenager, he and Arlene spent a fortune enjoying raw fish all over Tokyo. In retrospect, the Skippy looked cheap.

But it was his visit as a preschooler that we always laughed – and cringed – about.

We'd taken a Shinkansen (bullet train) down to the ancient imperial capital of Kyoto. Unlike so many other Japanese cities, Kyoto emerged largely unscathed from World War II – Washington had removed it from its atomic bomb target list because of its cultural significance – and remains a delightful surviving relic of the era of the shoguns.

By sheer luck, we were there at the height of the *sakura* (cherry blossom) season, a festive time when the Japanese go out en masse to party in the parks under the beauty of the fragile blooms. We promptly joined the thousands of Japanese tourists at the Imperial

Kabuki Flying

Getting ready to take Morgan on Japan's Shinkansen bullet train (top) and checking out the local food (right)

165

Palace Park, a gorgeous place dotted with small shrines, weeping cherry trees, manicured grounds and beautiful fishponds. It's particularly stunning in cherry blossom season, when millions of fallen blossoms form a smooth pink skin over the ponds and people travel from all over the country to see the special sight.

The heavy press of visitors forced everyone to walk slowly in a long, winding line along the paths, mostly maintaining a reverent silence that made it feel a little like a pilgrimage. It was a hot day, everyone was already sweating freely – and we seemed to be among the few *gaijin*.

Somewhere in the grounds, Morgan had acquired a forked stick that he refused to give up. He was already whiny and hungry when we arrived at a particularly beautiful pond, which had a low fence around it to keep visitors away from the water. Arlene and I were enjoying the tranquillity of the delicate display when a stick sailed over our heads and landed in the water with a loud splash. It made large ripples that instantly pushed a jagged wound into the once perfect pink surface.

The crowd of Japanese tourists gasped and looked around in horror to see who could have done such a terrible thing. Morgan started to scream that he wanted his stick back.

There was no escape. If we wanted to stop the overheated child from becoming even more hysterical, I had to fetch his damn stick from the pond. I stepped over the low fence – another unthinkable act to the Japanese – ripping open the leg of my pants as it caught on the wire.

Then in front of the aghast, air-sucking crowd (a sound Japanese make to show disgust or disapproval), I leaned over the bank and plucked the blossom-coated stick from the water. I scuttled back over the fence, leaving crushed blossom footprints in my wake. We left the imperial gardens as quickly as possible, leaving behind a royally ruined pond and an indignant crowd who had just seen their worst suspicions of *gaijin* behaviour confirmed.

166

Chapter 19
On the Line

Japanese airline managers fear the JCAB like nothing I've ever seen before. They treat government inspectors like gods of aviation rather than the typical bureaucrats who populate most regulatory bodies. Worse, many of the inspectors are failed pilots who revel in intimidating and finding fault with those who've made it to an airline.

As our first course continued and the JCAB checks grew closer, a sense of panic permeated the training section. We were shown a movie to prepare us for the coming ordeal. It showed two uniformed Australian pilots being questioned by a JCAB examiner and then giving a full weather and flight plan briefing before their simulator check. We quickly realised that the Aussies barely understood the material they were briefing on with such apparent authority. We quietly sniggered when the captain swept his hand knowledgeably over a weather map while referring to 'a cold front and all that other stuff'. But they got away with their babble because they looked serious and sounded like they knew what they were talking about. It was indeed a great training movie – just not in the way our instructors intended.

Before the movie, we'd started buying into the training-centre hysteria and angst. Now we knew how to play the game. The format for the check was well known: 40 minutes of oral questions followed by 20 minutes for weather and flight plan briefings. Then, after a brief break, we'd climb into the simulator, accompanied by six uniformed officials from the JCAB and NCA who would scrutinise our every move and utterance. 'Extreme pressure' does not adequately describe the experience.

The time limit for the oral test was set irrespective of how many questions were asked. Quick replies would mean more questions, but slowness in responding could sound like we were trying to waste time. We realised that because the JCAB inspectors were not at home in English, they mostly nodded along while listening for key words. The solution was to make your answers as long and wordy as possible with a few key phrases thrown in now and again. And never to try and help while another pilot was answering, as Japanese see interruptions as bad manners.

I am proud to say that during an oral test that was part of my captain-upgrade exams some years later, I managed a 25-minute answer to a single question, perhaps some sort of JCAB record, during which I repeated the phrase 'paradigm shift' at least four times. I wasn't sure what paradigm shift meant, but I was thanked by the inspector for a 'most complete answer'. He then asked another question that proved he hadn't listened to one word of my monologue. Not that I blamed him. We were all simply playing a game.

The weather and flight plan briefings could be practised until smooth and word-perfect. The trick was to not try and be clever by introducing an interesting new subject that the inspector might then ask about in depth, thus exposing your complete ignorance of the matter. My partner unnecessarily mentioned an erupting volcano in his briefing and was then asked to name all the active Japanese volcanoes. Oops!

The simulator check was the same program we'd been practising for a month. You simply had to perform it well and show good 'commandability', a Japlish (a Japanese version of English that often caused us great amusement) word meaning to bark orders in a loud voice without ever saying 'please' or 'thank you'. You also have to follow procedures to the letter. When I made a small error during a simulator check by cutting short a procedural hold once I'd been cleared for the approach – something completely acceptable at SAA – I was repeatedly grilled as to why I did it and had to explain in detail why it was safe to do so. Nevertheless, I had to repeat the manoeuvre with company checkers at a later date. I didn't make the silly mistake of thinking Western in the simulator again.

Real-life flying – what we called line flying – however, was a completely different story.

What was the main difference between the two styles?

As I've mentioned, Japanese pilots generally took a similar approach to every situation, while Western pilots were more flexible about adapting procedures to fit the circumstances. An illustration of this was two approaches I did into San Francisco, one with a Japanese captain and one when I was captain myself.

In both cases ATC vectored us onto a high downwind for the active runway and ordered us to turn base (towards the runway) when they had a gap in traffic – an ATC-sanctioned short cut if you will. It meant intercepting the glide slope from above instead of below as per normal procedure – not a big deal if you have good situational awareness and good visibility, which we had in both cases.

In the first instance, the Japanese captain repeatedly refused requests from the tower to turn until he was in a position to intercept the glide slope from below. Eventually the annoyed-sounding controller stopped asking and said sarcastically, 'You let me know when you're ready to turn, Nippon.'

When I was flying as a captain, I did the early turn safely and without problems – just as I'd seen lots of *gaijin* pilots do over the years. I think ATC's problem with the flight when I was the co-pilot with the Japanese captain was that when they heard my voice on the radio they assumed we were a *gaijin* crew and accordingly vectored us tight.

The trick with flying for a Japanese airline was not to attract attention by showing instructors a weak spot in your flying ability. If you did, they homed in on it like a laser and mercilessly drove you until you overcame it, gave up and resigned, or were fired. But if you didn't have an obvious weakness, they left you largely alone.

Once you were signed out onto the flight line to fly with other Western pilots, life improved greatly. In fact, it was so good that we came to think of NCA as our 'jumbo flying club'. You came to understand the unspoken system. In the simulator and on flight checks you flew in the Eastern manner – more of the kabuki play. On the line with *gaijin* pilots you flew the jumbo flying club. Those who didn't grasp this subtle point butted heads with the Japanese all the time and were ultimately terminated.

We *gaijin* were a diverse bunch. NCA had started recruiting outside Japan some years earlier as a fledgling outfit trying to expand its services beyond Asia. Planning to start international operations to America and Europe with five new Boeing 747 freighters, the company approached TWA, then a major US carrier, to supply pilots and run American flight operations. I was told by some of my colleagues that TWA wasn't really interested in what they saw as a nuisance contract and quoted a ridiculous price for their services in order to kill the deal.

To their undoubted surprise, NCA accepted anyway and their one-sided relationship began. NCA was milked for years by a complacent TWA management who came to believe that the contract was a permanent source of easy revenue. TWA failed to understand that the Japanese carrier was studying them and slowly gaining confidence in international freight operations.

TWA was taken by surprise when NCA suddenly brought in an international leasing group to supply non-US contract pilots like us. We were from all over the world, which meant that we had to get to know each other's styles at the same time as we got used to the Japanese way of doing things.

Some of these differences were already apparent during our

On the Line

*Feeling a little tired after one of my flights
as an NCA co-pilot*

My hard-earned Japanese flying licence

first course. We all let loose a little on weekends, but none more so than the Irish pilots. I thought I'd seen some serious drinking in the SAAF and SAA, but when the Irish got going, I realised I'd seen nothing at all.

When we South Africans said we were going out for the night, we meant we'd be back after midnight. When the Irish boys said they were going out drinking for the night, they meant they'd be back after sunrise after consuming quantities that would have put me in hospital on a drip. They'd stroll in after breakfast, looking shaky but still dressed in their evening finery.

More amazing, they'd be absolutely fine after a few hours of sleep. I promised myself that I'd never, ever get talked into going drinking with these guys.

The hard partying did have a price, though. At the end of our three-month course, most of us had saved about $5 000 in unspent meal allowance. The Irish pilots spent it all and more, settling their final bills with their personal credit cards. To a man, they considered it money well spent.

In spite of the influx of foreign pilots, NCA was a thoroughly Japanese airline. NCA training and maintenance was done under contract by then part-owner ANA in Tokyo, which also supplied them with Japanese flight crews and check pilots.

So why didn't NCA simply use Japanese pilots for all their needs? The answer is cost. As NCA wasn't state-owned, they could hire whomever they wished – and they wished to hire well-qualified Western pilots who were willing to work for much less pay than Japanese crews and without the hassle of trade unions or government-mandated pension funds, which would be required for Japanese pilots.

We never thought of ourselves as cheap labour, but to the Japanese that's exactly what we were.

When I joined NCA, we still saw some traces of Japan's 1980s bubble economy, a time when it seemed like Japan and Japanese methodology might dominate the world. Japanese companies always seemed to have money to burn and insisted on all types of luxuries. Even the paper cups, hot towels and stainless-steel cutlery on NCA aircraft were customised with a logo on everything – a complete waste of money on a freight aircraft with no paying passengers.

We saw remnants of that mindset when our ground school ended and we were introduced to our simulator instructors in an awkward little ceremony. After introductions, the whole group immediately went to a traditional restaurant for a formal lunch. We didn't order; elaborate food bowls just began to arrive shortly after we sat cross-legged on the floor. Slurp, slurp went our instructors on one side of the table. Chomp, chomp went the *gaijin* on the other side as we eyed each other across the table. There was little conversation and, surprisingly, no liquor, but right after lunch we were marched to the simulator for the instructors to check out our flying ability. A little alcohol would probably have helped everyone.

We had many of these lavish lunch spreads during our first course, most of which was left uneaten on the table. (That waste didn't stop my getting a reputation at the training centre because I'd turned down sashimi at a formal lunch. Weeks later I was introduced to an instructor I'd never met before and he immediately responded, 'Ah yes, Schapiro-san, no sashimi.')

When I did my last NCA course in Japan many years later, these ritual cultural interactions had disappeared. One reason was that NCA management had become more comfortable with foreign pilots and finally realised it was a waste of time and money imposing their cultural norms on us. Instead, they appointed a *gaijin* leader, to whom we and they could complain, and left us to our own devices, hoping we'd behave appropriately in Japan and not embarrass them too badly. In truth, everyone was a lot happier.

Another reason was that after Japan's financial bubble burst in the early 1990s, fiscal reality set in like a giant hangover. Companies began to trim away at waste and unnecessary expenditures. Gone were traditional lifetime jobs, regular salary increases and guaranteed bonuses.

NCA's decision to use 'cheap' foreign pilots instead of unionised Japanese aviators was part of that new austerity. So was purchasing plain paper cups for their aircraft. By the late 1990s, we began to see something new in Tokyo (but depressingly familiar in Western cities): beggars and homeless people living on the streets. Unfortunately, it only became worse as the Japanese economy stagnated.

When we first arrived in New York, fresh out of our NCA training, we were deeply resented by the NCA/TWA pilots. I heard that one moron actually complained to the US Department of Commerce that we were taking American jobs, forgetting that they were taking Japanese jobs!

They also tried to persuade their NCA pilot-manager that non-American *gaijin* were second-rate pilots who would crash their aircraft. Apart from causing severe anxiety for some Japanese, this unrealistic fear dissipated when they saw that we were easily the equal of the TWA pilots. I suppose the Americans were just defending their turf, but they didn't realise that the ground had already shifted under their feet and there was nothing they could do to change it back. Most calmed down once we began to fly together, and we got on very well. Within a year, the TWA contract was terminated and their pilots were released back to TWA, which eventually drifted into bankruptcy and disappeared.

Those who'd seen the writing on the wall had already resigned from TWA to stay with NCA.

Chapter 20
'Land at Nearest Suitable Airport'

I was with one of those former TWA captains on the rainy summer afternoon that we took off from Amsterdam to fly via the polar route.

This was the flight described in the Prologue, when the fire alarm sounded as we were high over the Norwegian fjords and the checklist told us our only option was to land at the nearest suitable airport. Painfully aware of what a fire on board had done to the *Helderberg*, I was flying on the clackers – the safest maximum speed – as we started to dump fuel and begin our descent into Bergen.

For the first time since the fire alarm rang, we had a few moments to spare. With time to think, the dull feeling in the pit of my stomach surged into open anxiety and I felt slightly nauseous from the adrenaline rush. I battled to keep my mind clear and bent down to tie my shoelaces to keep myself occupied.

The captain asked the flight engineer if he'd be willing to take an oxygen bottle and mask and have a quick peek downstairs. He came back to report no visible smoke but a strange, strong smell on the main deck. (It later turned out to be garlic!)

We were not out of danger yet. A corrosive or noxious chemical leak could still be the source of the problem, but at least there were no open flames. That would give us more time to prepare properly, as it was clear we'd still be overweight when we arrived over Bergen.

We had to decide whether we should land immediately and risk blowing tyres or circle Bergen to keep dumping down to landing weight. In the absence of visible smoke, we elected to do one more dumping circuit without going too far from the airport.

We circled at 3 000 feet just off the coastline, fuel spraying steadily from our wingtips. I noticed some netted enclosures beneath us and realised that because we were a couple of thousand feet too low for the fuel to vaporise in the air, we were dumping raw fuel onto salmon farms – a major industry in Norway. But environmental considerations have to take a back seat in an emergency like this. As we established the jet back onto final approach, the flight engineer ceased dumping and I realised something completely beside the point – I was still in my sweatpants and T-shirt. Well, at least I'd be comfortable for the landing.

I landed safely on the shortish runway and, followed closely by several fire engines, taxied the jumbo to a remote spot and shut down. I quickly changed into my uniform and went down to the main deck. We clambered over the cargo pallets closest to the detector that had sensed smoke, but it soon became clear that the fire warning was a

One of our checklists

Inside the cargo hold of an NCA freighter

false alarm, possibly caused by excessive moisture evaporating from plastic sheeting that had got soaked during loading.

We opened the front entry door, and after a short delay airport authorities towed a portable gangway to the aircraft. Two Norwegian officials came on board and the first thing they said was 'You don't look Japanese.'

It took eight hours for us to get back into the air. NCA insisted on crossing all the t's and dotting all the i's before allowing us to depart Bergen.

Actually, I'm understating it. When the NCA execs heard their plane was down in Bergen, they went crazy – but first they had to find Bergen on a map. The most level-headed was the Amsterdam ground engineer who picked up the phone and booked a seat on the first plane to Bergen. He knew he'd be needed to sign out the faulty detector and release the 747 for flight.

While we waited for him to arrive, Captain Mississippi and I were driven to the airport building to telephone our Amsterdam office. We reported exactly what had happened and asked for new flight plans to be faxed to the local operations office. We were then introduced to the airport staff, who were keen for us to stay the night in their town to sample their local beer and spirit.

Not so keen was an official from the Norwegian Civil Aviation Authority who was only interested in our fuel dumping. How much did we dump and where? Well, actually 100 000 pounds – more than 45 000 kilograms – right over your fish farms, but I figured he wouldn't appreciate that fact – especially if he was having salmon for dinner. Once he learned we hadn't dumped below 3 000 feet, he was satisfied we hadn't broken Norwegian air law and went away like a good bureaucrat.

We were driven back to our 747, where we began to receive a steady stream of airport visitors, attracted by the unusual sight of a giant freighter on their small apron. We gave them the Japanese-branded sodas and dry foods in our galley. They inspected the aircraft and went away happy with their Japanese-flavoured mementos. I kept thinking we should get out of town before they tasted their Japanese-flavoured salmon.

Other residents who'd spotted our aircraft circling or heard there was a strange jet parked at the airport began streaming out from Bergen to see what was going on. Our remote spot was close to the airport boundary fence, which backed onto rows of tall trees. Within a short while, the trees and boundary fence were full of people taking photos.

When it became apparent that we wouldn't be getting away quickly, we would have been within our rights to call it a day and stay the night in Bergen. In fact, if we continued, we would be well over our maximum duty time, something the JCAB took very seriously.

Three factors made us continue. One was that most of the freight was perishable goods from Amsterdam, such as flowers. These would have been ruined if we stayed the night. There was also the fact that we'd spent such a long time on the ground in Bergen that we could consider our time there as rest time and restart the time and duty clock. (I did, in fact, lie down on a bunk for a couple of hours.) More importantly, Captain Mississippi's wife was ill and he badly wanted to get home. As in most situations, the personal issue was the real deciding factor.

Exactly eight hours after our precautionary landing I dragged the thundering 747 back into the air – to the delight of the people who'd climbed up the trees to get a better look. Luckily, we didn't have to carry as much fuel because Bergen's shorter runway significantly limited our maximum takeoff weight. It would have been impossible to offload freight there without proper handling equipment. We said farewell and thank you to Bergen ATC and continued northward on our very long day.

Seven hours later, in Anchorage, at the foot of the gangway stairs, we were met by the Japanese station manager with very un-Japanese-like enthusiasm. He bowed repeatedly and thanked us for our dedication to duty. Then he promised us official certificates of thanks, a paid dinner and, finally, a cash reward. Now he was getting our attention!

I did indeed get a certificate, handwritten on special embossed paper in *kanji* (Japanese characters). I can't imagine what it must have cost them. Or what it says.

Sadly, no dinner or cash turned up. While Japanese pilots are typically expected to carry out difficult duties without question or expecting a bonus, exceptional efforts did get a monetary reward from the airline.

This actually happened to a few *gaijin* pilots in the early days too, but as NCA became more familiar with foreign crews, the company realised it wasn't necessary any more. *Gaijin* didn't expect to be rewarded for doing their job well, so if we weren't offered anything extra, we wouldn't be offended if we didn't get it.

So even though we were offered, we didn't get it. And of course I was offended.

Chapter 21
Challenges and Routines

People often ask me if I got scared flying. I did. But not for their imagined reason. I once saw a movie about Project Mercury, the programme that put the first American astronaut in space. American rockets were still dangerously unreliable, with one test capsule blowing up on the launch pad and others experiencing technical failures. The movie shows an astronaut sitting strapped into his tiny capsule atop a Mercury rocket and saying a small prayer. 'Please God,' he prays, 'just don't let me screw up.' That described my fear perfectly.

I always loved the challenges of flying – and there was certainly no shortage of them.

The first sector that I operated for NCA as a new co-pilot was to Chicago. The forecast at arrival time was for scattered thunderstorms, not uncommon in the summer. I asked the former TWA captain what to expect and he told me to relax. He said he'd been flying to Chicago for 25 years and assured me that the Standard Terminal Approach Route (STAR) arrival and approach would be unaffected by the weather. At worst, we might have to hold for a few minutes at the entry point.

Needless to say, it didn't quite work out like that.

When we approached Chicago, a series of unusual storm cells – isolated, instead of in a line – began moving across the area, causing havoc in the overcrowded airspace. First, ATC changed us from our western to a northern STAR. This required a couple of busy minutes to input new coordinates into the navigation computer. No sooner had we finished and set heading to our new entry point than they changed us to an eastern STAR! We were being bounced from point to point like the steel ball in a pinball machine.

While dodging thunderstorms en route to our newest entry point, ATC cancelled the eastern STAR and gave us radar vectors instead. Chicago had just changed runways, a major undertaking at peak traffic time. Now seriously busy, we hauled out new runway charts and studied them briefly. We kept avoiding cells to the left and right until eventually we were established on final approach with a strong, gusty crosswind and some wind shear – rapid variations in wind speed and direction – promised right down to touchdown.

We were on short, short finals when the gusty conditions forced the jet ahead of us to miss his turnoff. The tower ordered us to go around! I jammed on the power and lifted the nose while the TWA captain raised the gear and set the flaps. Round we went and were vectored on a wide left-hand circuit to reposition for another approach.

I was enjoying myself hugely.

The captain kept repeating that none of this had ever happened to him before in Chicago. True, it was the strangest weather I would see there for the next 15 years, but going around was a common feature of ultra-tight Chicago flight operations. I would do many more of these circuits in the years to come.

I would also develop a much-practised routine for trips to and from my different destinations. Jet lag was a constant problem that I never really got over in all my years of flying. It's worst when you fly due east or west, and being bored and awake when everyone else is asleep can lead to trouble.

Once, as a much younger pilot in SAA, I had a few crew members in my New York hotel at 2 am We'd eaten, bar-hopped, eaten some more and were looking for something to do. Someone thought it would be a good idea to drape ourselves in my bedsheets. It might have been me. Soon we were running up and down the corridor in sheets with holes poked through for our eyes. We decided to wake up the co-pilot and his girlfriend. We took the emergency stairs to his floor, where we found a water-filled fire extinguisher. He was sensibly suspicious and only opened his door a crack, but it was enough. We blasted his room out with the extinguisher before he managed to slam the door shut.

It was going so well that we wanted to share the wet-down with other crew members. The screaming and door-banging attracted hotel security. They came running and we fled into the stairway, dropping the used extinguishers, which clanged noisily down the concrete steps. As we climbed clumsily in our sheets, we could hear the security guys following one floor below. Amazingly, we all got back to my room without being caught. My bed was ruined, the sheets were ruined and, worst of all, I still wasn't tired.

I'd stopped running around emergency stairwells by the time I was flying as a captain. Instead, I'd developed an unvarying flight routine for each destination we visited. Here, for example, is a typical flying day out of Anchorage:

The beeping of the electronic alarm in my Hilton hotel room drags me out of a light, restless sleep, the only kind you get when you're chronically jet-lagged. This is followed almost immediately by the telephone ringing – my backup wake-up call. I lift the receiver and replace it immediately in the cradle, the accepted signal that a pilot is already awake. The clock glows 3.30 am.

I resist the strong urge to close my eyes again, a seductive trap that I fell into once before, with disastrous results. Instead, I stumble towards the bathroom and begin, on autopilot, my much-practised process of getting prepped for a flight.

Exactly 30 minutes later I open the hotel room door, feeling barely more awake than when I first got up. Showered, shaved, bags packed and neatly dressed in a freshly ironed uniform shirt and navy-blue uniform, with my battered blue Delsey suitcase in tow, I leave mumbling a thank-you to the room for a good night's rest.

In some ways I've become a little like my Japanese colleagues. I notice how they deeply respect and often thank the equipment they rely on. It seems like a fine idea, and, anyway, what's to lose?

The door slams firmly shut behind me in response. I always try to be the first crew member down at reception. As captain, you like to herd your crew along without being obvious about it. I recognise the crew driver dozing in a comfortable lobby chair. As soon as the final crew member appears, we make our way to the little white crew bus.

My copilot on this trip is a no-nonsense ex-SAA pilot who joined NCA a few years after I did. There are some co-pilots I don't feel confident about leaving alone in the cockpit, even to go to the bathroom. He is not one of those. Our flight engineer is a lanky American with the habit of finishing a huge bowl of free bar popcorn every night without ever putting on weight. As someone who blows up from just thinking about food, I have to admire that.

We walk out into the bite of an Alaskan winter. It's snowing lightly, with a cutting wind and good few inches of the white stuff already on the ground. The quiet crew bus putters carefully through the frozen, deserted streets. Too early for chatter or joking, the crew prefer to doze. As Anchorage is possibly the best snow-removal airport in the world, I'm not concerned about our getting out on time. Anyway, if there was going to be a planned delay, airline operations would've stopped us leaving the hotel or at least warned us about it the previous night.

Before long we see the familiar long row of airport lights. We stop at a security checkpoint and pass our crew identification badges forward to the driver to hand over for inspection. Once through, we're driven to a low, dark building some distance from the passenger terminal. As NCA is a freighter outfit, we operate

In the captain's seat – always on the left of the cockpit – for NCA

An Anchorage stopover

in the unglamorous working sections of the airport unseen by the flying public. This suits us just fine.

I step carefully out of the vehicle into the trademark soft slush of an Alaskan airport apron, a gooey mixture of ice and antifreeze fluid with a paste-like consistency that consumes a pair of flying shoes each year. We pass through the heavy, soundproofed door into the brightly lit flight operations centre, with its familiar stale-coffee smell. One by one, we place our labelled suitcases on the departures luggage rack and drift over to the dispatcher waiting patiently behind the counter with a neat stack of printed documents spread out before him. We briefly examine the documents to make sure everything looks correct for our flight.

The flight briefing specified by NCA is formalised down to each pilot's having a designated place to stand when receiving it. The captain stands in the centre, the co-pilot to his left and the flight engineer to the right. The only time I ever saw this pecking order changed was when I was captain-in-training and allowed to stand in the privileged centre position. To try it on for size, I guess.

The Japanese take this formal, ritual stuff very seriously. For example, each aircraft has a religious lucky charm in a special envelope sealed with a bow. Mess with it at your peril.

We signal our readiness to the tired-looking dispatcher and he begins his briefing. What follows is a detailed description of the coming flight, including weather conditions, active runways, aircraft weight, takeoff calculations, fuel requirements and the exact route and altitudes we'll be flying to Japan. I nod along with the briefing, but my mind is mostly in neutral. Sometimes the briefing gets more interesting, if one of the numerous volcanoes on our route is erupting, or there is bad weather, ATC problems or aircraft malfunctions. Mostly it's the same routine stuff.

When I first joined SAA in 1979, flight dispatchers actually calculated long-range flight plans line by line, a task that could take hours. Now, data is crunched by a computer half a continent away and printed out wherever it's needed. Dispatchers simply rip the completed flight plan from the printer, check it over and make a few copies. Uncertainty is not a desirable trait in aviation, and modern flight planning is deadly accurate and reliable compared to the old manual days.

Secrets from the Cockpit

The dispatcher finally stops talking and, grateful for his silence, I sign in two places to accept the documents. He picks up his copy and turns away, signalling the briefing is over. I'll sign at least a dozen times more before this flight is over. The co-pilot gathers up the thick stack of papers and we trudge back to the crew bus. After a short ride in the frigid gloom we arrive at the foot of a steel gangway pushed up to the front left door of our blue-and-white 747 freighter. Our careful climb up the perforated steel steps is punctuated by the piercing whine of the jet's air conditioning unit and the staccato warning horn of a moving pallet loader.

On my way up, I glance at the leading edges of the wings and the gaping engine nacelles. If they are already coated with fresh snow, I make a mental note that we'll definitely need de-icing before departure.

I often remember being taken to the engine maintenance shop during my initial training course at SAA. I'd been stunned by the sheer size of the jumbo's turbofan engines compared to what I was used to in the SAAF. It was actually possible to stand upright in their huge nacelles – something air hostesses often did for promotional photos. On later visits to the hangars, I'd see how the same giant engines seemed dwarfed by the bulk of the jet itself. Someone once called the 747 'aluminium overcast over a sea of wheels'. The label fits perfectly.

We step through the entry door into the brightly lit, skeletal fuselage, its steel floor dotted with rollers. Far to the back, we see huge plastic-wrapped pallets being loaded through the rear cargo door. They skate over the floor rollers into their designated position and are then firmly latched in place.

A narrow, somewhat shaky aluminium ladder rises between the pallets, leading to the upper deck. We climb up with practised ease, our flight bags in hand. Fresh coffee, brewed by the Japanese ground engineer in anticipation of a sleepy crew, perfumes the warm upper deck, which, unlike the main cargo deck, is indistinguishable from a regular airliner. It consists of the cockpit, a stainless-steel galley, bathroom and 16 plush business-class-style seats for passengers authorised to travel on the freighter. Behind the seats is a curtained crew rest area with two hard bunks that are surprisingly comfortable.

We wait patiently for the ground and service personnel to unblock the narrow entrance to the cockpit and galley and then ease our way forward. I enter the carpeted cockpit and slide my flight bag onto the metal shelf next to the left-hand seat. Then I roll the seat back and ease myself onto its sheepskin-covered fabric. I always felt instantly at home in my familiar 'office', surrounded by myriad controls, gauges, switches and a colourful array of warning lights.

The 747 cockpit is surprisingly compact, as all controls and switches have to be within easy reach of a seated crew. Apart from taxiing, or the few rare moments in flight when the jet's shadow is visible on a cloud or on final approach, the pilot is oblivious to the size of the aircraft and simply flies this cosy nook through the skies. The rest of the plane follows happily along.

First things first. I unknot my tie, roll it up and stow it next to the heated windscreen. I won't put it on again until we're in Japan. Then I drape the seatbelt ends loosely over my lap, slide the seat forward and set my seating position using the 'eyes level' markers as a guide. It's especially important in poor weather to sit correctly in order to have proper outside visibility. Finally, I wind the rudders forward until I can push them to their full travel distance.

I learned to fly in the SAAF on North American AT-6 Harvards, 1930s-generation airplanes built in the USA to train World War II pilots. A popular joke then was about the difference between British and American aircraft. The British, it was said, build an aircraft and when it's finished they poke a small hole in the fuselage for the pilot to sit in. The Americans first get an armchair and then build an aircraft around it. The Harvard had two pilot seats in tandem, but the cockpit was indeed sized for corn-fed American farm boys. I needed two cushion pads behind me to achieve full rudder input.

The enormous Boeing 747 was made for pilots of all sizes, so I didn't need to fly with cushions any more. Interestingly, each pilot seat feels slightly different in every 747. A minutely higher glareshield or a tiny rake or tilt to the seat makes it easy or impossible to find the perfect spot for comfort and vision in each individual jet. I was rarely satisfied with my seat position.

Cockpit preparation is a team job so the co-pilot and I work our way systematically through instrument checks, warning systems, programming the navigation and flight management systems and setting up the Standard Instrument Departure (SID) route. We normally divide the flying sectors equally between us, but we've got an extra leg so we're going to share this flight. I'm going to do the takeoff and the co-pilot, who won the coin toss, will do the landing in Narita.

While the flight engineer is still occupied with his more detailed and complex system checks, we slide our seats back and head to the galley for a much-needed jolt of caffeine. I gulp down a can of over-sweetened Japanese orange juice and follow it with milky coffee. Then we relax on the comfy seats, eat freshly loaded cheese rolls and complain to each other about the early hour until the engineer steps back with the aircraft logbook.

I study the jet's maintenance history and, if satisfied with its serviceability, sign to accept the giant machine. Unlike some other airlines, maintenance issues are rarely a problem in meticulous NCA.

When loading is finished, the snow-speckled loadmaster appears with another batch of documents to sign. The co-pilot and I peruse the load manifests, load sheet, weight and balance document and finally the dangerous goods list. Under strict packing and loading conditions, a freighter may carry many goods forbidden on passenger aircraft, including nuclear materials. It's not as dangerous as it sounds.

Challenges and Routines

I sign, sign and sign yet again. Then it's 'See you soon' to the locals and 'Sayonara' to the Japanese personnel as the engineer follows them down the ladder to check that all doors are properly closed and latched. Newly energised by the coffee and snack, we make our way back to the cockpit, strap in and put on our headsets. I give the co-pilot a nod and he calls ATC with our flight details. They confirm our SID route and advise that we can start engines when ready. We hear the upper-deck hatch thumping shut and the flight engineer settles back into his seat. Another nod and the co-pilot begins the before-start checklist. When it's complete, I establish interphone contact with the ground engineer and advise him to commence de-icing operations.

De-icing is a two-stage process. First, the whole jet is sprayed with a high-pressure jet of hot water to clean off existing ice and snow. This is followed by a coating of special anti-ice solution to the wings and tail to prevent ice build-up on those critical areas. It always sounds and feels like we're in a giant car wash as hot spray drums onto our windows and fuselage. It takes 15 to 25 minutes to prepare a 747, depending on how much snow is on the aircraft and if one or two spraying units are used. I always feel sorry for the guys doing the de-icing, perched on the tip of a moving gantry and fully exposed to the weather and blowing anti-ice droplets.

When the ground engineer calls us to advise de-icing is complete I note the time and call for the co-pilot to start engines 4, 3, 2 and 1 in sequence. He stretches to the overhead panel and flips the starter switch for engine number 4. I observe the giant engine starting to rotate and when it is at the correct rpm I move the fuel cut-off lever to give it fuel and ignition. The engine accelerates and at 50 per cent N2 – the engine compressor rotation speed – the co-pilot releases the switch and begins the start sequence for the remaining engines. When all engines are started, I dismiss the ground engineer and send him back to his office with a wave.

Taxiing is one of the few times when you really feel the size of the 747. It's delicate, tricky work to taxi a giant jet in the dark on a frozen, snowy apron with partially obscured markings. A normal rule of taxiing is to use either power or brakes but never both at the same time. We were also supposed to ensure that the jet never stopped in the turns. But on a slick, snow-covered surface, power against brakes is often the only way to control your speed and to avoid juddering to a halt on a sharp turn. This balancing act is one of the hardest parts of the job, but also one of the most rewarding if you do it well.

Normally, we run out takeoff flaps as soon as we begin taxiing, but on a snowy day we leave them tucked in the wings until we approach the runway to avoid icing them up. Then we quickly extend them, run the before-takeoff checklist and depart as soon as possible. As we near the runway threshold, the tower clears us for takeoff. With the checklist complete and adrenaline flowing nicely, I line up carefully down the runway, steering the nose wheel just to the left of the illuminated centreline to prevent it bumping annoyingly on each light during the takeoff roll.

The co-pilot and I confirm the runway heading to ensure we aren't on the wrong runway, something that can happen quite easily under adverse weather conditions. I push the thrust levers forward and stabilise the four engines evenly at a low setting. When satisfied, I engage the auto-throttle switch, which opens them smoothly to full power. As the engines accelerate, the cockpit fills with the characteristic buzz-saw sound emitted by the big turbofans. The jet surges forward and the centreline lights begin to blur beneath the nose as we gain speed. Soon they merge into a fluid stream of light. The co-pilot calls 'V1' (no stopping now!) and then 'Vr', our time-to-fly speed.

I lift the nose of the jet to the calculated pitch angle, and with a small bump we're airborne. 'Gear up,' I order. The co-pilot reaches forward and lifts the landing-gear handle to the up position. The landing gear rumbles into the wheel wells as the last airport perimeter lights disappear beneath the nose. Now there is nothing outside but blackness, so we concentrate on our flight instruments as the huge jet hurtles into the frozen darkness.

An airliner after takeoff is a wallowing, ungainly flyer, hanging narrowly onto flight by its high body angle and high thrust of its engines. As soon as we reach a safe altitude, I lower the nose slightly to begin accelerating the jet. As the speed slowly increases, we retract wing flaps in stages. Within a few minutes, the wings are clean and we climb strongly over the mountainous, volcanic terrain towards our initial cruise altitude.

Passing 12 000 feet, I engage the autopilot, release my shoulder straps and relax back in my seat. The cockpit is quieter now, the loudest sound the rushing of air over the curved, heated windscreens. As we proceed on course, we're passed from one ATC controller to the next. More than 30 years of piloting instinct tell me everything is going well. When I get the opposite feeling, I do a careful cockpit scan, often finding some small detail we've missed. Sometimes, if a flight is going really well, endorphins flow through your body and the enormous flying machine begins to feel like an extension of your fingers. You feel what it feels and, to some extent, man and machine become one.

Once we pass 24 000 feet, the jet climbs free of the solid overcast with a few shimmies and shakes and the polar night sky comes into view. It's impossible to be indifferent to this stunning sight. Free of city lights and the dust of the lower atmosphere, billions of glowing stars are visible from our panoramic front-seat view. An added treat is that on this flight the aurora borealis, or northern lights, is active. We watch diaphanous curtains of green and white neon flashing across the sky, disappearing and reappearing in shimmering waves. Being able to view this heavenly light show, unseen under the solid overcast, is fair compensation for getting up so early.

The jet ascends slowly to the thin, bitterly cold altitudes where we'll spend the bulk of the flight. The outside temperature is a frigid −65 °C, but it's warm in our heated, pressurised tube. However, if you press a damp cloth onto the steel windscreen frame, it instantly freezes itself onto the metal. We sometimes use this trick to hang sunshades.

The ghostly hand of the auto-throttle gently tugs the thrust levers back as we reach our preplanned altitude. Once settled in the cruise, I verbally hand over control to the co-pilot and head back for a well-earned cup of tea. Then I shed my uniform, pull on dark sweatpants – the same colour as my uniform, but somehow the Japanese could tell the difference between sweats and formal pants – and head back to the cockpit with a diet soda and large apple. I'm never comfortable wearing a jacket and tie, and this informal comfort and the help-yourself galley are what I love best about flying freighters instead of passengers.

I never wore a long-sleeve shirt in the cockpit as I overheat very quickly, especially when the sun bakes into the cockpit at high altitude. In general, too, flying is an adrenaline-laced business and the cockpit can be a sweaty place. Even if nothing unusual is happening, a pilot is pumped full of action hormones at least twice on every sector, on takeoff and landing.

Boeing supplied removable green tinted screens for sun-side windows, but the true lifesaver was an eyeball vent that blew a stream of cold air directly at you. You could love or hate a plane for this little vent alone. On 727s and early-model 737s they were small passenger-type vents, but the 737 advanced model had a giant eyeball that could pound you with cool air. It was eyeball heaven. To my delight, NCA's later-model 747s had both electric seats and giant eyeballs.

At this point after takeoff there is little to do except to monitor the instruments and radar, fill in the flight log and report to ATC as we progress on course. I settle back into my seat, verbally assume control and send the co-pilot back to take a long break and a leisurely breakfast.

Challenges and Routines

The jet drones on, seemingly suspended in space but actually moving at Mach 0.85 (85 per cent of the speed of sound). The cockpit is a beautiful place at night, with the muted glow of hundreds of switches, controls and instruments. I always feel completely relaxed in this *Star Wars*-like setting and I wonder for the umpteenth time how it is possible that a Jewish boy from Cape Town with an unlikely dream of flying could end up in this most un-Jewish of jobs: in the command seat of a Japanese-owned Boeing 747 high above the North Pacific Ocean heading for Tokyo.

Chapter 22
Coffin Corner
and Cockpit Cockups

Most airline pilots share a simple philosophy. Do your best, don't take unnecessary risks, learn from your screw-ups and never repeat them.

And then there's the rare other kind who believe they're always right because they know better than everyone else. They never learn from their mistakes because in their own minds they never make any; all the screw-ups they're involved in are always someone else's fault. Such pilots are stressful to fly with, and it becomes more and more difficult for an airline to find pilots willing to fly with them.

One such pilot was an ex-Royal Air Force captain hired and subsequently fired by a number of international carriers, including NCA. But for a few years we had the dubious pleasure of his company in NCA cockpits, where he ran up a string of dangerous and costly incidents. None of which were his fault, of course.

After one five-day trip with him during my co-pilot years we had so many close calls that I refused to fly with him again. In fact, it almost convinced me to go back to SAA.

Here's what happened.

Day 1: Anchorage to Amsterdam – a close encounter

Captain Know-It-All and I were preparing to take off from Anchorage on an overcast spring afternoon. We were headed to Amsterdam via the polar route and our Boeing 747F was at its maximum takeoff weight for the nine-hour sector. The captain was the flying pilot to Amsterdam. We received our takeoff clearance, rolled down runway 06R and became airborne. The SID required us to fly straight ahead until passing 2 000 feet and then turn left, climbing to 6 000 feet. We entered cloud at 1 500 feet and were in IF conditions after that.

About 16 kilometres away from Anchorage International is Elmendorf Air Force Base. The main runways at both airports are roughly parallel to each other and they operate on different tower frequencies.

When we began our left turn at 2 000 feet, our new heading would take us directly over the air base. All military traffic was supposed to be well below us by then.

But on that cloudy spring day, a formation of four F-15 fighters were arriving for weapons training at Elmendorf from the 'Lower 48', as Alaskans call mainland USA. While we were getting airborne at Anchorage International, they were positioning for landing at the military base. The F-15 formation had been instructed by Anchorage approach to descend below 3 000 feet and to contact Elmendorf tower for landing instructions. They contacted Elmendorf but for some reason remained at 3 000 feet, possibly because they were unfamiliar with the area and still in cloud.

Our Boeing 747 was now going to be in the same airspace as the F-15s at exactly the same height, in cloud and on different radio frequencies. Not a good situation, to say the least!

No sooner had we begun our left turn than ATC advised us about possible F-15 traffic crossing below us and asked if we had visual contact with the fighters. ATC believed that the F-15s had already left 3 000 feet and expected us to be well above them. I told them we were on IMC in cloud, and although there were a number of aircraft indicated on our Traffic Alert and Collision Avoidance System (TCAS) screen, none were displaying as conflicting traffic. ATC was now satisfied that the F-15s were not an issue, but we were still in a climbing turn and not yet on our new course. As soon as Captain Know-It-All levelled the wings on our new heading, the

TCAS instantly showed a bright yellow dot, indicating conflicting traffic 800 feet above us.

TCAS is a modern system installed in aircraft cockpits to help avoid midair collisions. It gives pilots a visual display of their aircraft's position and its vertical separation from other traffic. If TCAS senses a possible conflict, it upgrades the encroaching aircraft's display from white to yellow and then to red. Yellow gives an aural warning ('traffic, traffic'), and if the situation worsens, the warning is upgraded to red. At that point, about 16 seconds before a possible collision, an aural and visual resolution advisory (RA) is given for action a pilot must take to avoid an impending collision. Pilots are required by air law to comply with the RA, which takes precedence over ATC instructions. The system expects the pilot to react correctly within five seconds of getting an RA, giving ample time to avoid a collision. It is extremely dangerous to ignore or not fully comply with an RA as the conflicting aircraft will also be getting an RA from their TCAS – but in the opposite direction.

It took just a few moments for the yellow F-15 traffic advisory to change to a red RA. 'Reduce climb, reduce climb,' it chanted in an urgent mechanical tone. The flight instruments lit up with the required RA prominently displayed on the vertical speed indicator (VSI). All we had to do was follow it in order to stay safe.

But Captain Know-It-All saw the situation differently. As we were already climbing, he wanted to climb a little faster to clear the traffic. This was perhaps possible in a Royal Air Force fighter but impossible on a maximum-weight 747 with takeoff flaps still set. He ignored the RA and instead pulled back on the yoke. The speed instantly started to decay (decrease) because there was no extra thrust available to sustain the higher climb rate. By now TCAS had sensed the worsening situation and changed the RA to an urgent 'Descend, descend, descend'. The red F-15 traffic dot began to merge with our position on the TCAS screen.

Unbelievably, Captain Know-It-All was still in a climbing

frame of mind, but the heavy 747 had run out of steam. Belatedly, he pushed the stick forward but succeeded only in going level at 3 000 feet, the same altitude as the F-15s. He didn't actually descend at all.

I kept looking at the TCAS screen and it showed a terrifying picture: the red traffic dot and our position now merged with 0.0 altitude difference between us. It meant we were right on top of each other.

There was no point in looking at the TCAS screen again. It couldn't show anything worse. Despite being in heavy cloud, I looked out the window, waiting for the impact that must come at any moment. With our fuel load, altitude and speed, a collision would be disastrous for us and anything on the ground below.

At that tense moment, we suddenly emerged from the clouds to an unforgettable sight: we were number five in a four-ship formation of F-15 fighters. Our 747 was so close to jet number four that I could see heat stains around its tailpipe and read the yellow jet-blast warning plaque. They were in a slight left bank, slowly descending and turning away from us. Within moments, the danger was past and the TCAS warning went blank. The entire incident, from the first TCAS warning, was over in less than 30 seconds.

We sat in stunned silence in the cockpit, no one saying or doing anything at all. Then Captain Know-It-All started to scream about how ATC had fucked up. I felt a surge of anger so strong I had to restrain myself from physically lashing out. I decided to be professional and to delay a confrontation until we were on the ground in Amsterdam.

We reported the frightening near miss to ATC and continued on to Amsterdam. The flight passed in sullen silence, Captain Know-It-All busily composing his own report to NCA management. In Amsterdam, when we calmly discussed what had happened over drinks, he steadfastly refused to accept any blame for the near miss. Like many people with a truculent personality, he was actually quite good company off the aircraft or when he was getting his way. I started to warm to him a bit. It didn't last very long.

Day 3: Amsterdam to Anchorage – navigation insanity

Due to a slight delay with the crew bus, we got to our 747 a little later than usual for our Amsterdam departure. It was no big deal, but Captain Know-It-All instantly made it one. He made me cut short the loading of the navigation computer to try and save a few minutes – a recipe for disaster if I ever saw one. Arguing with him only made it worse, and the tension rose in the cockpit. It was now obvious to me why this guy had so many problems on his flights; he constantly set himself up for trouble.

Luckily, our departure from Amsterdam was uneventful. On a later flight from Amsterdam, it didn't go quite as well for him. Inadequate loading of the INS system caused a navigation system failure after takeoff that couldn't be corrected in flight. When he suggested to his crew that they continue over the North Pole anyway, they sensibly rebelled and demanded to return to Amsterdam. This screwup, which he blamed on the ground engineer, cost NCA hundreds of thousands of dollars in dumped fuel and other costs.

After cruising peacefully over the polar region for a couple of hours, Captain Know-It-All turned to me with a smile and an outrageously stupid suggestion. 'Have you ever done real polar navigation?' he asked. 'Let's give it a go.'

Before INS navigation, polar flights required a special grid overlay map and procedures because compasses are unreliable at such high latitudes. The gyro-stabilised INS platform didn't need a compass to navigate, but we had a special manual compass procedure in the unlikely event of our INS systems becoming inoperative in the polar region. This emergency procedure was what Captain Know-It-All was proposing we do, something no pilot in their right mind would suggest. What if we could not re-establish INS navigation after the exercise? We would be royally screwed. Why even take such a stupid risk?

A memory flashbulb went off in my head. I once took a flight out of Anchorage that this captain had just brought in from Amsterdam. During the preflight checks, I was puzzled to find the gyro compass controllers in manual instead of auto mode, a position no pilot ever uses – except, as I now realised, for flying manual polar navigation, which had not occurred to me at the time. So this moron had done his polar navigation trick before and had forgotten to reset the compasses afterwards, an omission that could cause major problems in a bad-weather approach. Luckily for him, they'd arrived in fine weather.

Instead of answering his request I said, 'Captain, let me tell you a story.' I related my experience of finding the compasses still in manual mode after his flight. I had barely finished when he started yelling, 'It wasn't me. I didn't do it,' and turned away to face his side window. There was no more talk of polar navigation after that. I sat back, satisfied that I'd saved myself a few hours of high anxiety.

It was a brief respite: there'd be worse anxiety when we departed Anchorage for Chicago the next day.

Day 5: Anchorage to Chicago to JFK – coffin corner

Anchorage lies on a coastal plain almost surrounded by mountains. Our flights stopped there because of its strategic location on some of the shortest air routes between North America and Asia. Use of the international airport by passenger planes declined after new aircraft types were able to fly longer ranges without needing to refuel and Russia opened up its airspace after the end of the Cold War. Even so, Anchorage remained a major cargo hub, with a heavy volume of daily freighters.

The tight apron was a magnet for incidents, especially in winter. I once saw a Korean Air 747-400 with its wingtip firmly embedded in the tail of Aeroflot 727. Also two 747s with their wingtips joined together. Someone got fired for those two incidents, for sure.

Secrets from the Cockpit

Despite getting more snow annually than most other airports, Anchorage's runways were rarely closed in the winter due to their extensive and very competent snow-clearing programme. I have never seen its like anywhere else in the world, least of all at New York's JFK airport, which sometimes felt like it could be closed down by three snowflakes blowing across a runway.

In spring, strong easterly winds can produce dangerous turbulence close to the mountains around Anchorage. In general, pilots like to use a runway facing towards their destination, as taking off in the opposite direction can waste a lot of fuel in a large airliner. However, under these turbulent wind conditions, even pilots heading east prefer to use the northwest runway because it allows them to safely gain altitude over the ocean before turning back over the mountains.

It was just such a windy day on this fifth day of my trip with Captain Know-It-All, but as the Automatic Terminal Information System (ATIS) was broadcasting the northwest runway for all departures, I was not concerned. Then he made a stunning request to ATC. He asked to use the runway towards the mountains instead of the northwest runway in use. My heart sank and I thought, 'God, he just never learns.'

I started to argue, but as before, it was no use. I pointed out that a Japan Airlines (JAL) 747 had recently lost a flap segment in just such conditions, but he stubbornly insisted that it was wasteful to use the northwest runway. An aircraft flies within a performance envelope that defines its flight limits. It cannot fly outside this envelope, which is broad at low altitude but narrows to a point at high altitude – also known as Coffin Corner. Narrowing the envelope means reducing your options, something no cautious pilot does unless necessary. Yet this fool was doing it again.

I considered refusing to fly, but as it was within his legal, if inadvisable, right to request the runway change, I'd be blamed for any delay. I decided to go along, telling myself I would never fly with this guy again.

We took off and at 2 000 feet, as per the SID, turned right to parallel the mountains while we accelerated to raise the flaps. Within moments of turning, the turbulence hit us, a gut-wrenching blow that jolted the whole plane. Then another hit as we lurched from turbulent wave to wave. I began to fear for the flaps when I noticed we'd stopped climbing for some reason. This was bad, as only altitude would get us away from the worst mountain turbulence.

Suddenly the Ground Proximity Warning System (GPWS) began to chant, 'Don't sink, don't sink,' as our much-needed climb now turned into a descent. I immediately called out, 'We're descending,' and Captain Know-It-All screamed back, 'I know we are. I want to get the flaps up quickly.' I sat back, stunned. This dumb fucker was descending on purpose! Having led us down this blind alley, he was now compounding his fuck-up by descending into vicious turbulence while surrounded by tall mountains.

Indeed, ATC suddenly became concerned about our poor climb performance and turned us away from the mountains until we'd gained some altitude, so we ended up heading in the wrong direction anyway. Once we were well above the mountains and back on track, I sat back in a cold, anxious sweat. I had never flown with such a dangerous captain in SAA.

We flew on towards Chicago in silence, the tension thick in the cockpit. I had heard from other pilots that this was the normal situation with this captain. Now I fully understood why. The sun set behind us and the cockpit became dark except for the softly lit instruments. As I didn't have to see the fucker's face any more, I began to relax, sensing my ordeal was almost over.

O'Hare International Airport is one of the busiest in the world. Seen from the air at night, it looks like a brightly lit hive with hundreds of fireflies buzzing around it. We were arriving fairly late, so it was a little quieter than usual. Like most major airports, Chicago has parallel runways, but as it's an older airport, some runways are a bit too short for comfortable 747 operations – especially at max landing weight. It's not that they can't be used, it's just that envelope thing again. Why reduce your options if you don't have to?

One such shorter runway is 27R. Its partner, 27L, is no problem at all; 747 pilots routinely request to use 27L when both runways are available. ATC knows this and generally gave us 27L anyway, even if we forgot to ask. In addition, 27L was a short taxi to our freight apron area; the other runway requires a complicated taxi route that can take 20 minutes or more. Using 27L was a no-brainer – unless you were Captain Know-It-All.

Approaching Chicago, the ATIS was broadcasting runway 27R in use. As we were at maximum landing weight, I asked the captain if I should request 27L. 'No,' he responded, '27R is fine.' Here we go again, I thought, but yet again, as captain and pilot flying, he was legally entitled to his choice. Besides, 27L might not be available as Chicago often closed runways at night for maintenance.

We began our descent. Our final approach speed that night would be 160 knots – almost 300 kilometres per hour – giving us zero margin of error for stopping on the shorter runway. We needed a perfect landing from a far-from-perfect captain. My adrenaline was already starting to pump when ATC called us to advise that 27L was now available. I sighed with relief and was about to respond affirmatively when the captain ordered me to tell them we still wanted to use 27R. 'What?' I spluttered, but he pressed the radio transmitter himself and told ATC he was requesting 27R.

I sat back, resigned. Yet again, this dumb fuck, who never, ever learns, had set us up for trouble. This had become a trip from hell, needlessly flirting with disaster on every sector.

Although Captain Know-It-All's decision-making was deeply flawed, he was actually a good pilot. He landed well and we stopped without a problem. The taxi to our apron from 27R took almost 30 minutes due to closed taxiways. We consequently blocked in very late, thus already stressing him out for the next sector. Who knew what bad decisions that would lead to? The thought that I would be flying the last leg was the only thing that at least gave me a modicum of comfort.

The leg to JFK was blissfully uneventful, and as I stepped onto the New York apron, I thanked God it was over. Captain Know-It-All went straight to the manager's office to begin making excuses for his Anchorage debacle.

I went straight to the roster clerk who assigned flights and crew pairings.

'George,' I warned the amiable man, 'I'll never fly with that guy again. Not as co-pilot or as passenger. If you can't manage to arrange that, I'm going back to SAA.'

George sighed and pulled out a notebook from a drawer in his desk. He opened it and added my name to the long list of pilots who'd preceded me.

Chapter 23
Time Travel

Jet lag was a constant issue in our lives. All NCA flights were east to west, which meant our bodies were always out of sync with our physical location. As we kept on moving, we never really caught up.

When I started flying for NCA in 1994, the fastest route from Tokyo to Amsterdam was over the North Pole via Anchorage. We'd routinely fly the polar route over the unique world of the frozen north in both directions, about nine and a half hours from Anchorage to Amsterdam. We'd look down on the vast, desolate expanse of northern Canada, scattered with lakes frozen over for much of the year.

But the really stunning sights were in Alaska. There we flew over hundreds of glaciers, billions of tons of compressed ice pouring their unstoppable mass into lakes or the ocean in an ultra-slow-motion tableau. Equally impressive were vast flat plains of snow and cracked ice, all that remained of ancient mountains ground down over aeons by the relentless movement of glaciers.

In Anchorage, at 61 degrees north, the difference in sunlight between summer and winter months was startling. In midsummer, residents enjoy 18 hours of daylight and six of darkness. In winter it's reversed; they endure 18 hours of frigid darkness and just six of weak, watery sunshine, the sun barely making it above the horizon before disappearing.

I discovered that on a polar flight during winter, it's possible to see four sunrises and four sunsets in a single day. Here's how it worked on a flight from Alaska to Amsterdam.

Time Travel

The sun rises at midmorning in Anchorage – our first sunrise. We're driven to the airport in the early afternoon for our flight. As we're taxiing out for takeoff, the sun sets – our first sunset.

We climb to altitude, heading north. As we climb, the sun rises again due to our increased horizon (sunrise two). Once we settle into the cruise, it sets again (sunset two).

A long, dark night over the pole. Then, just before we descend into Amsterdam, the sun peeps over the horizon again (sunrise three). As we descend, it sets due to our reduced horizon (sunset three). We land in Amsterdam in the dark. As we're driving to the hotel, the sun rises again (sunrise four). Later in the afternoon, we see it set for the fourth time in a 24-hour period.

Another interesting phenomenon was crossing the international date line, running from the North Pole to the South Pole, at 180 degrees east/west – the exact opposite of the Greenwich meridian, at 0 degrees. This is how it would work on a flight from Anchorage to Narita and back to Anchorage:

The flight departs Anchorage at 6 am on Tuesday morning and flies seven hours to Tokyo's Narita International Airport to arrive at 7 am, more or less the same time of day due to time-zone changes. But Tuesday changed to Wednesday when we crossed the international date line heading west, so now it's Wednesday morning, not Tuesday!

The crew stays at Narita for 36 hours and departs at 9 pm on Thursday evening for Anchorage. We fly through the night and arrive in Anchorage at midday, not on Friday but on Thursday! Because we crossed the date line heading east, we get to enjoy Thursday all over again.

Because of this phenomenon, you can enjoy two birthdays or two New Year's parties, or, if you're unlucky, none at all.

If you did a couple of trips back to back, you invariably arrived at the 'sleep graveyard', an unhealthy state where your sleeping patterns became a series of three-hour naps interspersed with marathon 12-hour crashes. In short, you became a mess.

Narita airport is 13 time zones away from New York. We flew there at least twice a month, but because we only stayed for 36 hours there was no point in trying to adapt to the new time zone. Like most NCA pilots, I simply lived on modified New York time.

A typical stay at Narita meant we usually touched down around 7 am and taxied our 747 to an allocated bay on the freight apron. My flight always felt incomplete until we received a deep bow from one of the Japanese marshallers, something they routinely did after we shut down. Everywhere else in the world, marshallers mostly just strolled away. I liked the bowing.

By 8.30 I'd be in my hotel room, feeling tired from the flight. I'd read the *Japan Times* in the bathtub and then stroll to a local superette to get something for that night's breakfast, normally bread and cheese. For some reason, it was almost impossible to get wholewheat bread in Japan without going to a specialist *gaijin* store. The closest thing I could find in a regular supermarket was white bread with a few wheat grains tossed in as an afterthought. At about 11 am (10 pm the night before, New York time), I'd close the curtains and go to bed after setting my alarm for 7pm (6am in New York).

When the alarm went off I'd force myself to get up and stagger downstairs to catch the hotel bus to the town of Narita. The bus was full of walking zombies like me. I'd return a couple hours later on the same bus and collapse into bed again, slightly tipsy and nicely full after dinner at one of my favourite spots.

By midnight I'd be shifting restlessly between the sheets, and by 1 am (noon in New York), I'd be up for good. I'd switch on all the lights and TV and scan the *Japan Times* again. If I was lucky, there'd be a couple of subtitled movies to watch. If not, the TV stayed on a Japanese channel as background noise while I ate the unhealthy superette breakfast and drank many cups of milky tea.

I'd be awake until the sun rose four hours later. In the hot, humid Japanese summer, sunrise was the only time you could jog without dissolving into a pool of sweat, and I was only too happy to get out of my little cell. After the jog I'd shower and cool down for a while, then head out for a 50-minute walk to Narita via the back roads. Narrow, bamboo-lined paths wound prettily between rustic farmhouses and their terraced rice paddies. I loved watching the year-round cycle of rice farming and the little creatures that had adapted to living in the paddies. There were abundant yellow-and-black-striped spiders that grew to enormous sizes and scared the hell out of me.

The back road passed directly below the approach path for Narita runway 24R, and with a westerly wind half a dozen giant jets might pass a few hundred feet above my head as I strolled.

On one such day, a FedEx MD-11 passed noisily overhead. It grew quiet again but a minute later, there was a rushing, whistling sound and the bamboo trees lining the path started to sway wildly. I stopped to ponder what had just happened. Two 747s roared by, followed by an Airbus A340. The trees stayed still. Then another MD-11 passed overhead, followed again by that eerie sound and the wildly rocking trees. I had read somewhere that the MD-11 generates particularly vicious wake turbulence. Here I was actually hearing and seeing that wake turbulence striking the trees like a mini-tornado – an incredible and rare sight.

For much of the time I flew there, Narita was an unfinished airport. Protests by farmers and radical students that began in the 1960s over the government forcing local residents to sell their land to make way for the new airport had blocked the planned construction of its second and third runways. The protests had soon escalated into violence. The demonstrators tried every trick in the book – sledgehammers, petrol bombs, bags of manure – to stop the airport being built. Once that strategy failed, they tried to stop it being used. There were pitched battles with police. Thousands were injured or arrested; at least five people – three police officers and two demonstrators – were killed. At least one farmer hanged himself. In one notorious incident, riot police beat unconscious an elderly woman who refused to give the government her land, and used their riot shields to carry her away.

After the new airport opened in 1978, it looked like a fortress, with tall fences, checkpoints, watchtowers and armed police patrols. The farmers responded by erecting tall bamboo towers next to the runways to prevent safe flight operations. These structures often sprang up overnight.

When I started flying into Narita in 1994, only one of two parallel main runways were in use; the other was still blocked by legal and physical obstructions. But what fascinated me most was a small, fenced square of land smack in the middle of the concrete apron with a few fruit trees growing in it. It was the last remnant of the last holdout farm on the operational side of the airport. Then, between one flight to Japan and the next, it was suddenly gone, replaced by smooth concrete. I wondered if maybe the owner was also gone, also under smooth concrete?

The farmers, however, were not gone. Along with left-wing activists, some of them turned to sabotage and terrorism. Once, during an early-morning jog, I came across one of the armed police patrols deployed to stop them. These were not your friendly neighbourhood cops. After checking me out carefully, they grimly indicated with their weapons and attitude that I should fuck off quickly. Which I did.

These police needed to be grim. On 3 February 1998, three homemade rockets landed in Narita's cargo area. Two landed and exploded in the paved area near the hangars, scattering fragments and injuring a cargo handler. One actually rolled under the tail of an NCA 747 but didn't explode. Kakurokyo, a left-wing group opposed to Narita's expansion, later claimed responsibility.

Some reports said the rockets had been fired from a bamboo grove half a mile from the airport. But we heard they'd come from a small truck parked in the lot of the hotel closest to Narita. This was an ultra-modern complex we called the Ghost Hotel because we never saw anyone actually staying there, except for Canadian aircrew (which might be saying the same thing). We'd always speculated that the hotel was a front for something illegal, maybe Japan's mafia-like organised crime gangs known as *yakuza*.

Hotel staff always parked their cars in the small staff lot on the airport side of the hotel, which likely would have allowed the attackers to park their truck unnoticed. The rockets, concealed in the canvas-covered back of the vehicle, were timed to go off later that evening when the airport would be busiest. The closest part of the airport to their truck happened to be the freight apron, where our aircraft were parked.

The story we were given was that the rockets were angled too low because the parking lot wasn't level and the shortened trajectory didn't give them enough time to arm themselves in flight. Whatever the reason, it was a close call for Narita airport. For the Ghost Hotel, it was a gross abuse of staff parking rules.

I didn't come across any anti-airport activists, but I did see some less attractive sights on my Narita walks. Once out of eyeshot of the main roads, residents would dump their unwanted possessions anywhere. Garbage and abandoned appliances, even motor cars, littered every ditch and were rarely picked up. They were simply left to rust away.

After my walks I usually had a lunch of chilli pepper soup and a mixed salad at my favourite Korean restaurant. They knew their *gaijin* aircrew customers were on a different time schedule, so they were already open for lunch at 10.30 am. Occasionally, I'd force myself to go someplace else, but then I just wished I'd eaten the chilli soup instead.

I'd be ready for bed again by the time I got back to the hotel, where I'd pack my hard-shell Delsey suitcase and hit the sack until the phone rang about 7 pm for call time. I never set an alarm in

Narita as the airline would update our call time with the hotel depending on our flight's estimated time of departure. A porter would come by exactly 30 minutes after call time to collect luggage from outside the door. No tip was ever required; in fact, it was considered an insult to offer one.

I'd always buy a can of cold coffee in the lobby shop to kickstart me for the flight. The stuff was so dense you could stand a spoon up in it. I preferred cans of hot or cold Royal Milk Tea during the day, but the caffeine-laced coffee was a real eye-opener before a flight. An NCA driver and van would be waiting for us at reception for the ride back to the airport and flight operations. It was tempting to drive off as soon as your crew was downstairs, but it was best to wait for the exact hotel departure time in case there were some dead-heading crew getting a repositioning ride to operate a flight from another airport. Leaving someone behind was a constant source of friction, but after official hotel departure time, they were on their own.

Once back on the aircraft, we'd set up the cockpit while the caterers and cleaners finished in the cabin and then pop back to eat a snack from the galley to get our blood sugar up. A typical snack at Narita was three delicate sandwiches with two pieces of melon, a slice of orange and three grapes on the side. Yes, three grapes! But they were huge Muscat-type grapes with soft black skin and a melt-in-your mouth flavour.

Even if we would have preferred more grapes, the Narita snack was infinitely preferable to the nasty sandwich tray that was routinely loaded for us in New York. It consisted of the worst that Western food can offer – cheap processed meats on stale white bread and dry rolls seeping with watery tuna and a viscous yellow mayonnaise that was as likely to make you feel sick as satisfied. The sandwich tray was a constant source of jokes ('You'll be sent a tray every night by NCA as a retirement gift') and one aspect of New York that everyone hated. No matter how many times we ignored or cursed the disgusting tray, it never went away.

Chapter 24
This is Your Captain Speaking

When I joined NCA as a co-pilot in 1994, the airline warned that there was no programme to upgrade us foreigners to captains. Three years later, they decided it was better policy to promote foreign co-pilots they were familiar with than to hire unknown captains. Better the *gaijin* you know, I suppose.

It meant another upgrade course in Japan, where once again I'd have to spend a few months away from Arlene and Morgan in New York. Luckily, Ray, another ex-SAA co-pilot I'd known since my boy pilot days, was also on the course. A softly spoken, universally liked gentleman, Ray's calm demeanour impressed our Japanese upgrade simulator instructor, who once compared my flying style unfavourably to Ray's, describing him as a 'Gaijin Buddha'. (Ray ruined that impression one morning in the simulator by being so badly hung over that he did a circling approach without saying a single word, a procedure where you normally don't stop talking. Gaijin Buddha indeed!)

We took our instructor to our favourite Japanese eatery, The Red Lanterns, which he contemptuously dismissed as 'Korean' the second we walked in the door. In return, he took us to his club. I've no idea what the evening cost him, but when we entered, we were each handed a cup full of imitation dollar bills. 'For what?' I asked. 'You'll see, Schapiro-san,' he assured me.

We sat at a small table and, after a short while, a tall honey-blonde girl wandered over and sat herself down. I was chatting to the beautiful young lady, who claimed she was Canadian, when she stood up in mid-sentence and whipped off her robe. She was completely naked underneath. I couldn't keep the surprise off my face, so she whispered, 'I have to do it or we can't keep talking – they're watching us on video.' Clearly hungry for conversation in English, she sat very close for the cameras while she told me how she'd been recruited in Canada to work the lucrative Japanese club circuit. Unlike the other girls, though, she said she had a plan. 'Another year,' she claimed, 'and I'll go back to my home-town and purchase a horse farm. No one will ever know where the money came from.'

I saw small needle puncture marks on both her arms and knew that her dream would never happen. But, always a sucker for a good story – and to our instructor's obvious dismay – I handed her my entire cup of notes.

Day by day, week by week and flight after flight, the upgrade ordeal of training and intensive study to prepare us for the dread-ed JCAB check dragged on. Being stuck in a small hotel room far away from our families, it was easy to go a little stir-crazy, so I decided one afternoon I needed a companion in my hotel room. (But definitely not the club girl.)

I'd seen small live red crayfish for sale at the fishmonger that I thought could make excellent, if unusual, pets. I only wanted one, but as they were sold by weight I had to buy 200 grams' worth. That meant three of the little clawed critters. I took them back to my room and put them in a little water on a small circular tray with a raised edge. The crayfish remained where I'd placed them, barely moving.

Perhaps they were hungry, but what could I feed them? I went downstairs to the hotel shop and examined the snacks available. I chose a packet of dried squid, cut it into tiny shreds and put it out on the tray. The crayfish instantly became interested and started snacking. I realised that Japanese people and crayfish enjoyed the same food, so feeding them would be easy. They were still barely

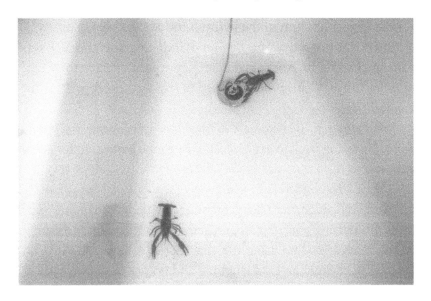

My new pets make themselves at home in the tub.

moving in the tray, but as it was getting late, I switched off the light and went to sleep.

I woke up with the uncomfortable sensation that someone else was in the room. I listened. Suddenly there was a scuttling, clicking noise. I switched on the bedside light. The floor was alive with the crayfish, out of the tray and rushing around, clicking their oversized claws at each other. They spotted me looking at them and raised their claws threateningly. Holy shit. I stared at the frightening sight and stayed on the bed until morning.

Next morning, I decided to thin out the herd. I rounded up the hiding crayfish and took two of them to a nearby creek, where I released them. I later realised I'd probably just ruined an expensive eco-programme to rid the creek of alien species.

I named the survivor 'Claw' for obvious reasons.

Claw lived on his tray during the day and in the bathtub at night. He ate so much squid that he began to moult from his shell. Ray promised to look after Claw while I was flying, but

I think he just left him in the bathtub the whole time.

Then the big day came for our JCAB upgrade check. I was scheduled to fly to Anchorage and Ray would operate the flight back to Tokyo. Our instructor, wise to my ways, prepped me for the flight.

'Schapiro-san,' he began. 'You must stay in your seat the whole flight. No going back to eat or sleep. Just to the bathroom for a few minutes.'

'Okay,' I responded.

'And,' he added, 'no taking off shoes or tie, no changing your pants, no putting your feet up, no standing on the seat, no sitting on the armrest and no using the checklist as a sunshade. Also, no sleeping in cockpit, no loud laughing and no reading newspaper or books. You just fly.'

'Okay,' I responded.

Unfortunately, I had to get rid of Claw before I left Japan. I took him to a friendly NCA office worker who'd once invited me to her parents' home for dinner. (But only once, as I immediately screwed up by walking in with my shoes on – a big mistake in Japan.) I handed her Claw in a small plastic bowl along with his bag of dried shrimp. 'Please don't eat my family,' I pleaded, thereby irrevocably insulting her.

She accepted Claw with a small bow. It was a sad little ceremony, but unlike Claw I was almost free.

Strangely, the check flight that transformed me from a 747 co-pilot to a 747 captain was an anticlimax after the months of build-up. But it was thrilling to be in charge of a jumbo jet and there were certainly plenty of thrills in later flights.

With the end of the 20th century approaching, scare stories about a coming electronic Armageddon were building up. What would happen to computers when the year switched from 1999 to 2000?

This is Your Captain Speaking

In order to save memory space, early-model computers had been programmed to use only the last two digits of the year. That meant 1980, for example, was recorded as 80. Did Y2K, as the problem was dubbed, mean that computers would think 2000 was really 1900? Would they shut down or malfunction because they thought they'd gone back in time?

Around the world, people had started preparing for wide-spread disaster. On aircraft, malfunctioning onboard computers could cause engines to shut down, navigation systems to go dark and radios to stop working. NCA decided to ground their whole fleet at Narita before midnight on New Year's Eve. That way, they could safely test their machines and repair them all at once if something did malfunction.

I flew into Narita on the morning before Y2K to find the airport already packed with aircraft. Rows of 747s from ANA, JAL and NCA lined the maintenance areas. Later that day, they started to park arriving machines on unused taxiways. We waited in our hotel rooms with bated breath for midnight. After all the growing hysteria, and with our imaginations fuelled by saké, the least we expected was for the hotel lights to go out as Tokyo's power plants ground to a halt. It was like waiting for the end of the world – except that nothing happened, other than it took two days to clear all the parked aircraft out of Narita airport.

One of our American flight engineers had so bought into the lurid predictions that he'd stashed a month's supply of canned food and bottled water in his cellar. After Y2K, he made himself eat tinned stew for a week as punishment for being gullible and gave away the balance to a food bank. In truth, there were many people who should have been eating canned food that week.

As I've said, I never missed the time I'd spent flying an aircraft full of passengers. Our cargo could be interesting in its own right, and I enjoyed the occasional conversations with those who needed to accompany items, such as the museum curator who flew along to keep an eye on priceless artworks being loaned out for an exhibition.

There were also animals that needed special care. We often flew racehorses between New York and Japan and could tell from the smell as we walked out to the jet when horses were aboard. They were put in special metal stalls that were secured on the main deck for their attendants to check on them during the flight.

Some horses were placid travellers, but others didn't take to the air so well, especially if there was turbulence. They'd kick the stall with their back hooves, causing resounding thumps that resonated throughout the jet. They normally calmed down after a few hard kicks; if they didn't, an attendant could give them a tranquilliser shot. We always feared that an out-of-control horse might kick its way out of the stall and then right through the aluminium fuselage – although I never heard of that happening.

More rarely, we also flew stud animals to Japan. I once got on board in New York to find an enormous bull glaring at me from a modified stall. I asked the young male attendant sitting upstairs if, like the horse minders, he had a syringe to tranquillise the bull if necessary.

Surprisingly, he did not.

'Then how are you going to calm the bull if it gets stressed?' I inquired.

He shrugged. 'Feed it, I suppose.'

'But it's a stud bull,' I teased. 'It doesn't want to eat! You'll have to get into the pen and let it have its way with you. Next time you'll rather bring along a syringe.'

Or not, I thought unkindly, walking into the cockpit.

Chapter 25
At Cross Cultures

Even after I'd worked for a Japanese outfit for years, cultural misunderstandings persisted.

When I first arrived in Tokyo in 1994, we'd marvelled at how the maroon-coloured commuter train that we took to and from the training centre every day always arrived exactly on time – with the doors opening precisely at their platform-marked spots. Commuters who'd been deeply asleep moments before knew exactly when to rise and exit in one continuous movement. (We found out later that in this pre-smartphone era they would set tiny pocket alarms to vibrate just ahead of the train's scheduled arrival. The punctuality of the service did the rest.)

We also noticed that these riders always subtly separated themselves from us *gaijin*. No matter how full the train, there were always empty seats around us. Some stared openly at the un-Japanese hairiness of our chests and arms. When our nerves were getting frazzled deeper into the course, we occasionally amused ourselves by unbuttoning our shirts to give the gapers a better view. I once rudely grabbed four hanging straps on a crowded train to see if anyone would complain. The strapless passengers looked on plaintively but seemed too embarrassed by my loutish behaviour to ask for one.

Occasionally, there were official lunches with NCA management and weekly drinking sessions with senior instructor pilots in tiny backstreet bars. At one such bar, a tipsy woman asked our instructor (in Japanese) to ask us (in English) if she could touch our hairy chests. Of course we said yes and she went home after endlessly bowing her thanks. We agreed afterwards that she could at least have bought us a drink first.

We also had to learn to deal with Japanese plumbing. Our Japanese hotel rooms always came with a water-jet toilet – a type of under-the-seat bidet that is now quite widely available, but which back then scared the crap out of us Westerners. Given that the instructions for use were only in *kanji*, presumably even the manufacturers didn't expect *gaijin* to try it – except one morning I did.

I'd got up at 1 am and, unable to face the bright bathroom light, sat down in the dark. My hand accidentally brushed the toilet control panel. There was a soft whirring noise and suddenly a hard stream of warmed water squirted onto my backside. My eyes went from half closed to saucers in a split second. I leaped off the toilet and scrabbled for the light switch.

A powerful jet of water shot across the bathroom until the mechanism sensed its occupant had abandoned the seat. The jet quickly subsided and a little mechanical arm I'd never seen before retreated coyly under the rim like a spider waiting for its next victim.

As bad as those high-tech toilets were, traditional Japanese toilets were worse. Unlike a seated Western toilet, a traditional Japanese toilet is a standing affair with hash-marked pads for your feet and a long, smooth trough between them. Users squat as low as possible to do their business, aiming carefully for the trough. Once you are finished, you open a faucet to wash away the result.

Westerners typically avoid like the plague this modern version of pooping in the woods – usually not a problem because public bathrooms in Japan typically offer both types. Unfortunately, some traditional eateries do not.

I had eaten something that disagreed with me on my trip to Kyoto with Morgan and Arlene. As if Morgan's destroying the tranquillity of the cherry blossoms hadn't been enough, that trip also forced me to have my first experience with a squatting loo.

Unable to find a public bathroom, I'd scuttled off to the facilities in a beautiful wooden restaurant that had just opened for lunch. My heart sank when I found a traditional toilet in the single stall; I panicked further when I realised that squatting toilets were better suited for people wearing kimonos that could be pulled around their waists. What was I supposed to do with my pants to keep them out of the ghastly trough?

All I can say is I did my best. But it wasn't good enough.

Cultural misunderstandings persisted in the cockpit too.

As the era of three-person 747 crews started coming to an end, aircraft with two-person flight crews began to dominate. ANA, which supplied Japanese crews to NCA, made a decision to terminate their classic 747 passenger fleet. They retrained their 747 pilots on other machines, but it was the end of the line for ANA flight engineers. For their last few years of service, they were seconded to NCA, where they were forced to do the unthinkable: fly with *gaijin* pilots.

It wasn't unpleasant flying with Japanese engineers, just a lot quieter. Deeply marinated in Japanese cockpit culture, they did their job perfectly, sitting in their seats staring at their panel and saying nothing unless spoken to. After a few flights, though, they began to realise no one cared what they were up to and started to relax and even enjoy themselves, maybe for the first time in their careers.

Still, lifetime habits were hard to throw off. On a flight from Anchorage to Chicago with a Japanese flight engineer, I did my party trick of buying and preparing roast chicken in the galley oven for the crew. We sat in the cockpit with our trays on our laps, munching away at the delicious crispy meal. As usual, there was plenty of chicken left over. The engineer happily accepted my offer of another helping.

He had just begun to eat it when I decided I was full and put my tray on the floor. To my dismay, he immediately stopped eating, took all our trays to the galley and dumped his half-eaten chicken in the rubbish bin. I cursed my mistake. In the strict hierarchy of a Japanese cockpit, when the captain is finished, the meal is over for everyone. Obviously, we didn't care if he continued to eat, but once I signalled by putting my tray down, he instantly ended his own meal. I should've waited until he was finished eating.

Very occasionally, I got away with my Western sense of humour.

In New York our roster clerks were American, but our senior management, administration, pilot manager and flight checker were all Japanese. We noticed that the longer the Japanese staff stayed in America, the less rigid and easier to get along with they became. Unfortunately, no sooner had this happened than they were hauled back to Japan for a mind reset or were replaced, something I saw happen numerous times over the years.

One of our admin clerks was different. He seemed to prefer the old ways and remained stiff and uncomfortable with us *gaijin* even after he'd been in the US a while. Admin-san stuck to a very strict formula. If he said no, it meant no; if he said maybe, it meant no; and if he said yes, it meant probably not.

It was best to stick strictly to business with him, but after I'd been with NCA for a few years, I dared to ask him a more provocative question.

I'd been sleepily watching a TV programme in my Anchorage hotel room about the last days of World War II in the Pacific. Japan was using kamikaze pilots, who attacked enemy targets by deliberately crashing their planes into them – knowing that they'd kill themselves in the process. The programme included footage of the young men preparing for their final flights.

Each was given a ritual cup of saké before climbing into their Zero fighter planes. As they took off, the doomed pilots were bade farewell by a line of ground crew waving their hats above their heads in a circular motion. This piqued my interest, because I had seen that type of wave before. In fact, I saw it every time we departed from Tokyo. The Narita ground crew would line up on the apron and give us exactly such a wave as we took power to taxi.

These scenes made me a little uneasy. Did our ground crew also think we were on a one-way mission? I decided to question Admin-san on this usually taboo topic. I was sitting in the New York crew room at 3 am when Admin-san walked in to say hello. This was about as friendly as he got, so I started a conversation with a straight face.

'Admin-san, I have a question for you.'

'Yes, Schapiro-san, what is the question?'

'I saw a movie in Anchorage last week. Japanese pilots were preparing to fly. Before their flight, they each had a cup of saké.'

'Yes, Schapiro-san?'

'This is a Japanese airline. Why don't we get a cup of saké before we fly?'

There was silence as Admin-san pondered the ridiculous question. Then he nodded and replied with an equally straight face. 'Wartime only, Schapiro–san,' and walked back to his office. I was impressed. Perhaps there was hope for Admin-san after all.

Still, a misunderstanding with another Japanese flight engineer caused me some very uncomfortable moments. I was doing a check ride from San Francisco to Anchorage with a Japanese crew. The checker had a reputation as a bit of a tough case, so I studied un-usually hard for the flight. The midnight takeoff and departure from San Francisco went well and he asked one or two easy questions in the climb. Once in the cruise, the checker announced, 'No more questions,' indicating that the quiz phase was over, and ordered me to go back and rest for an hour. I was pleasantly surprised; this wasn't the hard case I'd expected.

As I left the cockpit, I asked the engineer to please call me in an hour. '*Hai*' (Yes) he responded. I quickly fell into a deep sleep. Later, I was woken by the engineer shaking my leg. I made my way sleepily back to the cockpit to find a royally pissed-off checker. 'You over time,' he hissed at me. I had no idea what he was talking about, but as I often didn't understand what the Japanese were say-ing, I just nodded and chuckled as if he'd made a good joke. He stiffened and left the cockpit, pale with anger.

I settled in and scanned the instruments and flight log. Something didn't look right with the flight times. I stared at the log and then at the clock. Eventually, I worked it out and my heart dropped. I hadn't been away for an hour. I'd been gone for three hours! No wonder the checker was so angry. The bas-tard flight engineer hadn't called me after an hour as he said he would. *Hai* indeed! I turned around and glared at him. He looked guiltily away.

Now I also understood 'You over time' and that I'd laughed at the checker when he said it. Shit, I was going to get it now. Trying to blame the engineer for my tardiness would only make my be-haviour seem worse. If he didn't confess on his own, I'd just have to suck up whatever came next. He didn't confess and I did get it. 'I can ask you any questions I like,' the checker spat at me upon his return and hit me with a string of obscure technical questions. My saving grace was that because I'd returned so late, we'd have to begin descending soon. I drew out my answers the way I'd done with JCAB questions when I first joined NCA.

Twenty minutes later, I began the descent. I knew I had better not screw anything else up, which is tough to do when the guy next to you is really hoping you will. Luckily, my fuck-ups were over for the day. After a perfect approach and landing, I taxied in and shut down. Nonetheless, I suspected that he might still fail my check flight. We sat in the passenger seats for a quick debrief.

'Schapiro-san,' he began, 'for your flying you get high pass but for your knowledge you only get low pass (minimum acceptable grade).'

It was meant to be a shameful rebuke but all I heard was 'pass', so I said, 'Oh, thank you, thank you very much' with a broad smile, leaving the checker to shake his head at the low standard of *gaijin* they'd hired.

I can't say that the Japanese didn't try with us, or at least put on a good show about it. Our onboard meals were supplied by the large ANA catering facility next to our hotel at Narita. Unlike our other international caterers, they supplied NCA with two different styles of food – Japanese or Western. Which type was loaded depended on which crew was flying the jet. We'd grown tired of having the same food choices out of Japan for many years. NCA decided it was time to change the menu when it realised that few meals were being eaten on board, especially not the one with the lurid orange sauce. I was in Japan on a Narita stopover and was politely asked if my crew and I could come to the ANA facility at 2 pm to pick the new Western-style menu. A Japanese crew would be there to pick the Japanese-style food.

The request was a nuisance, because at 2 pm we'd normally be trying to get some sleep before our evening flight, but I agreed in the interest of helping my colleagues.

The Japanese never do things half-heartedly. A large conference room had been laid out with examples of all the suggested meals. Numerous chefs stood by to offer hot samples. It was carefully divided into Eastern and Western offerings, and a Japanese crew was already working through the Asian side. After many years of flying and crew food, I knew exactly what *gaijin* were looking for on a tray. Within an hour, we'd examined the offerings. We made up six interesting rotating menus while the Japanese crew was still sampling soba noodles. Then we bowed to everyone and went back to bed, pleased with a job well done. I returned to Japan later that month and was looking forward to seeing which of our new choices had been loaded. I went to the galley to look at the new food and, to my shock, the lurid orange sauce – with some minor rearrangements – was staring back at me on the setup tray.

I found out later what had happened. Once the Japanese crew had made their own selections, they were asked to select the Western food. We were just there for window dressing and our selections had been ignored. We were used to being ignored, of course, but what pissed me off most was losing a few hours' sleep for the charade. And having to look at the orange sauce again.

I also learned the hard way that arguing about anything only made it worse.

On one lovely summer day in Anchorage, I'd hung up my jacket in the back, made my way to the cockpit and plopped myself in the captain's seat. Then I slid the electrically controlled seat forward to set the rudder pedals, keeping my feet well clear of the sides. Suddenly the seat gave a little jump and there was a sharp metallic crack. I looked down and saw the seatbelt strap lying across the seat track.

I cursed, pulled it out and examined the buckle. It had a hairline crack through the metal tip. I cursed some more and called the ground engineer, who took a look and went to find a spare strap. There wasn't one available, and I realised that my carelessness with the buckle was now going to cause a delay.

I looked around to see if I could improvise some sort of working harness. The cockpit jump seat had a seatbelt but unfortunately its fittings were different from the pilot seat. I devised a scheme using belts from both seats, which meant using two quick-release mechanisms instead of one.

The ground engineer examined my plan, sketched it and faxed the plan to Tokyo for approval. Ten minutes later we were in the air with a copy of the signed approval from Tokyo. We departed only five minutes late, with me resolving to be more careful with seatbelt straps in the future.

We landed in Chicago and taxied to our freight apron. There were three Japanese men in suits waiting for the aircraft – not a good sign. These suits came on board and one grimly informed me that I had broken US Federal Aviation Administration regulations with my seatbelt plan. American air law only allows one release mechanism.

'What?' I stammered. 'I had approval from Tokyo.' I showed them the stamped and signed sketch.

'No,' he responded, confiscating the sketch. 'Tokyo unapproved it during your flight. As captain, you are fully responsible for knowing all regulations.'

I knew a kangaroo court when I heard one, but I also knew that arguing was always a futile exercise.

'Okay, so I'm grounded?' I asked.

'No,' the suit responded. 'First you fly to New York. Then you're grounded.'

So we flew to New York, where the co-pilot and I were instantly grounded.

The Japanese take regulations very seriously, and the ground engineer got the worst of it. He was sent to Japan for ten days of retraining, which I suspect involved a lot of beer, saké and sashimi. I was sentenced to a day of retraining with the New York chief pilot, which meant lunch at a deli and a discussion about my 'crime'.

To the Japanese, the correct attitude for an offending worker is to fall on your sword without offering excuses and accept whatever punishment comes your way without complaining. That way, your problems go away very quickly. The Western method of arguing your case, including pointing out the hypocrisy of cancelling an approval in the air and then having to do a second leg after the cancellation, means your problems never go away.

I tried to argue for a few moments about the unfairness of my situation and instantly the chief pilot's jovial features froze into a stiff mask and he replied, 'Some in Tokyo do not agree.' My fate had already been sealed before our meeting. I bowed to the inevitable and advised the chief pilot I was fully to blame and would accept whatever punishment Tokyo dished out. The smile came back and he said my suspension was now over, but the incident would be noted on my record.

Secrets from the Cockpit

I was back in the air, but the truth is I felt the Japanese never trusted me in quite the same way again. And my nickname from then on among the *gaijin* crew was 'Captain Seatbelt'.

Chapter 26
Three-Engine Landing

What. The. Fuck! Instead of a nice clear screen, the radar screen was showing a mass of red thunderstorms.

It was my first flight back after being cleared for duty following sinus surgery. The operation, intended to address my worsening chronic sinus condition, hadn't quite gone as planned. Routine pre-surgical tests uncovered that I had a severe Factor 11 clotting deficiency. The condition, which is usually of genetic origin, meant that I had a shortage of the protein needed to stop abnormal bleeding.

The discovery explained why I'd bled so badly in the SAAF after having my wisdom teeth removed – and why this sinus surgery could be a problem. The surgeon addressed this by giving me a plasma transfusion before the operation, and Arlene drove me home later that day with my nose stuffed with packing. Apart from a little blood seeping out, it felt fine.

Later that evening, the trickle suddenly turned into a flood and blood began to pour out of my nose. Within a minute, my shirt was covered in red. Arlene rushed me to the emergency room and I eventually found myself in a hospital room with a plasma drip in each arm. The morphine I'd been given was starting to wear off and the inflatable stents that had been pushed into each nostril were hurting like crazy. Their pressure against my raw sinuses made it impossible to focus my eyes.

My companion in the room was a confused elderly man who was being prepped for some sort of bowel surgery. He didn't understand why his diet had been restricted, but he did understand that he was hungry and repeatedly pressed his call button to ask for food.

Hospital staff eventually brought a bowl of oatmeal to the room – for me. The old man stared at the oatmeal. I could see he really wanted it, but I knew I couldn't give it to him. I tried to eat a little, my head pounding. As I took a spoonful from the bowl, a watery discharge from my nasal drain dripped steadily into the oatmeal, turning it a reddish colour. The old man mumbled something and I turned to face him – he was staring at the red-tinted oatmeal and clearly still wanted it.

They discharged me later that day after the surgeon pulled out his torture balloons. I'd had another four units of plasma, one bowl of oatmeal and countless blood drawings until everyone was satisfied that my blood was now as thick as treacle. I went home to lick my wounds for a few days. My nose was so swollen that our neighbour's daughter started to cry when she saw me. That really cheered me up.

Now I was back in the air after being declared fit to fly by a New York flight surgeon.

I'd taken off from JFK airport and hand-flown the 747 to cruise altitude, where I'd just cleared the thin line of lights along the US-Canada border. In front of us lay dense darkness. I set the weather radar onto its 300-mile maximum scale. It looked clear, with not a cloud in the sky. The co-pilot was getting some rest and everything in the cockpit was set to my satisfaction, so I allowed my mind to drift as I idly watched the instrument displays for what I thought was a few moments. It was a mistake.

'ATC is calling us, Rob.' The flight engineer's voice jerked me awake and I sat up. 'They want to know which way you're going to turn.'

'Shit, I fell asleep,' I thought as I picked up the microphone to respond.

'Which way are you going to turn, Nippon?' the controller asked again. What?

I glanced quickly at the navigation display and flight instruments, but everything looked normal. Then I saw the radar screen. The display showed a mass of red thunderstorms almost at our aircraft! Where the hell did they come from?

A surge of adrenaline jerked me fully awake. I turned the radar scale to ten miles and saw that we were rapidly approaching a line of thunderstorms. It was too late to try and turn away, but I noticed a small gap between two of the cells ahead of us.

I instantly set the autopilot mode selector to HDG and steered the giant jet towards the gap, helping it with a heavy dose of rudder while calling for the flight engineer to switch on engine igniters and cockpit lights to prevent our being dazzled by lightning.

We entered the clouds and immediately were tossed around like a leaf. Lightning flashed on and off. I heard hail impacting on the windscreen and then, with a final series of shakes, the storm spat us out on the far side. The radar screen was clear for 300 miles.

Wow, that was close, I thought, my heart still pounding. I had never fallen deeply asleep in the cockpit like that before. Clearly the effects of surgery linger for longer than one realises.

The episode was not quite over. A Korean Air 747 following us in trail now called ATC to ask about the line of storms. 'Which way did Nippon turn to avoid,' the pilot asked the controller, 'to the left or to the right?'

'Actually, they seemed to go right through the middle,' ATC replied in a bemused tone.

'Okay, we'll do the same,' the Korean pilot declared.

It was a bad choice because the small gap we'd dodged through had closed up by then.

The Korean pilot called ATC three minutes later in a shaken voice.

'Aah, we are through the storms but was verry rough, verry

rough.' What an idiot, I thought. He didn't even have the excuse of falling asleep for flying directly into a thunderstorm.

The memory of that red-filled radar screen is with me as we depart Anchorage in poor visibility one snowy winter morning. After climbing steadily to our assigned altitude, we level at Flight Level (FL) 330 – equivalent to an altitude of 33 000 feet – for the long leg to Japan.

I take the first watch and my co-pilot Ed relieves me in the cockpit about three hours into the flight. I am dozing on one of the passenger seats when I hear 'Thump, thump, thump' and think, 'The damn horses are kicking again.' Then I remember that we don't have any horses on this flight. It is an engine barking! In the cockpit I see a perplexed-looking Ed and the flight engineer staring at the engine instruments.

'One of them is stalling,' Ed says in a strained voice, 'but we can't tell which one.' An engine stall is caused by disruption of the airflow through the engine. It can be very dangerous in a large turbofan.

I stare at the instruments and notice engine number 2's exhaust gas temperature is fluctuating a few degrees with every stall. 'It's number 2,' I say. Ed disconnects the auto-throttle and gently pulls back the corresponding thrust lever. As the engine decelerates to idle thrust, the thumping stops. It was maybe 200 seconds from the first stall to the last.

As flying pilot, Ed opens maximum power on the remaining three engines to compensate for the power loss and winds in some rudder trim to offset the unequal thrust. It's a temporary solution, because our weight means we'll have to descend shortly to a lower level. Right now we have other priorities. 'Should I shut it down?' Ed asks, his hand already on the fuel cut-off switch.

I ponder this for a moment. The Boeing manual says we should shut down a stalling engine, but it isn't stalling at idle thrust and the engine parameters look normal. 'Let's try putting on some power first,' I suggest.

Ed gently pushes the thrust lever forward and instantly a low vibration pulses through the jet. He quickly pulls it back and the vibration disappears. 'Keep it running at idle thrust for now,' I tell him. 'We can shut it down later if it starts to vibrate. You watch the speed and start a slow descent if necessary.'

After completing the emergency checklist with the flight engineer, I call ATC and advise them of our predicament. I add that we're not certain we can maintain FL330 and request a lower altitude if necessary. Anchorage ATC replies immediately: 'If you can't maintain altitude, you must turn off the airway. There is traffic below you that is too close. Let me know your intentions.'

Our intentions are to first see what will happen on three and a half engines. We know we'll have to descend on three engines, but will the extra one at idle thrust make any difference? It does. Our speed holds at FL330 and we can even reduce some thrust on the functioning engines.

I now have to decide if we should continue to Tokyo or return to Anchorage. We've not yet passed the halfway point known as PET (point of equal time), but Tokyo has perfect weather while Anchorage had snow with poor visibility when we departed. Also, Tokyo has maintenance hangars for a quick engine change. I decide it makes more sense to continue to Tokyo, and Ed concurs.

I advise ATC we'll continue to Tokyo at 330.

Other airliners on the NOPAC route system have been following our saga and begin calling us on the general communication frequency, offering to change their altitude or route if it might help. I thank them for their offers and explain that we're confident we can maintain altitude.

The truth is, no one else can really help you once you're airborne. In the air, your safety is 100 per cent in your own hands, but there's still a certain comfort in being offered assistance. We enter Tokyo airspace and sign off with Anchorage, who've already advised Tokyo ATC of our situation. Technically, we're flying on three engines after an engine failure and Tokyo gives us priority handling all the way to Narita.

It finally grows quiet in the cockpit. We've done everything we can to stabilise the situation, but I have one more sticky issue to deal with. We'd planned to share this sector and it's supposed to be Ed's landing in Tokyo. NCA regulations, however, specify that the captain must land the aircraft in an emergency.

I bring up the subject and Ed instantly hands over control of the jet. It's the mark of a true professional that he doesn't take it as a personal slur on his flying ability. What really convinces him is that I offer to buy him dinner for taking his landing.

The sky has been gradually lightening from behind and the cloud-covered Pacific Ocean is now clearly visible below us. Suddenly it becomes flecked with yellow light and shadows as the sun rises clear of the clouds. Morning has finally caught up with us.

The familiar pattern of northern Japan begins to display on the radar screen. The DME suddenly flickers into life as a Japanese radio beacon comes into range. When the distance to our TOD point shows less than 100 miles, I excuse myself and walk back to put on my uniform. Armed with a fresh cup of tea, I plop back in my seat, slip on my shoes and tie up the shoelaces.

This will be my first actual three-engine landing – something I've done hundreds if not thousands of times in the simulator. I decide to treat it exactly like a simulator exercise. Ed calls NCA ops on company frequency with our estimated time of arrival and they give him our expected parking bay. 'Mechanics will be waiting for you,' they advise. More useless assistance.

At TOD, I gently pull back the three thrust levers and the autopilot dips the nose to maintain the descent speed. Once fully closed, I reset the rudder trim that has been compensating for the uneven engine thrust.

With all engines at idle, thrust is even again but won't remain so for long. Every change of power, no matter how small, will need a readjustment of the rudder trim.

Airline flying is always like a 3D game of snakes and ladders, but never more so than on the descent. You need to know exactly where you are on that 3D game board in order to end up at a particular point in space at a particular speed. How you achieve it is the challenge and joy of flying. Failing to do so can have severe consequences. I've seen pilots who were already in trouble 60 miles from the airport but still let their profile get worse by not understanding where and why they were going wrong. It's all about energy management, really. How to gain energy, maintain it, trade energy or lose it. Once you grasp that, the rest is just easy maths.

ATC now turns us left to position our 747 for a long final onto runway 34L. Narita airport becomes visible in the haze beyond the Japanese coastline sliding slowly by on our right-hand side. The airport has a strange procedure on the approach to 34L. The landing gear has to be lowered before crossing the coastline, about five miles before the standard gear-down point, to avoid 'blue ice' falling off the aircraft. Blue ice is a reference to blue-dyed frozen toilet water. The procedure presumably originated after a plane's leaking toilet tank caused dyed ice that had built up under the fuselage to drop off when the pilot lowered the landing gear. The irate recipient of the frozen toilet water must have complained to the JCAB, which, desperate to appease the militant farmers, instituted this ridiculous rule that costs airlines thousands of dollars in wasted fuel every year. It's worth pointing out that the reciprocal runway, 16R, had no such limitation. Maybe those farmers appreciated blue water on their crops.

I wonder if they'll suspend the early gear-down rule for us. ATC says nothing, so I decide it's not worth getting involved in a complicated cross-language request. We have enough thrust to fly the standard approach with the gear down.

It's time to start reducing speed, which means we must first lower flaps. I call for flap 1 and Ed lifts the flap lever out of its up detent and slips it into the 1 position. Instantly, a rumbling is felt through the aircraft as hydraulic worm-drives begin rotating and drive the flaps out to their selected position. Simultaneously, pneumatic pressure pushes out a set of leading-edge flaps.

The flap warning light now turns green to show that the flaps are set. 'Flap 5,' I call, and we repeat the sequence until we have flap 20 and I can safely reduce to the JCAB-mandated approach speed. I open power to maintain the speed, being careful to leave engine number 2 in idle position and hold pressure on the rudder bar until I can wind in some rudder trim. We're approaching the coastline and I call, 'Gear down'. Ed reaches forward and slips the gear lever to its down position. The jet shudders gently as the gear doors open and the four giant bogies and the smaller nose wheel begin angling out of their wheel wells. They lock down, their rear wheels drooping. The gear doors close behind them and once again we have a green light in the cockpit.

Now we need raw power to fly level and maintain speed, an undesirable situation forced on us by the weird blue-ice rule and the reason it wastes so much fuel. But we're rapidly approaching the glide slope and as we capture it, I reduce some power to begin the steady three-degree descent that will end at the runway touch-down zone. Once settled on the slope, I re-trim the rudder for the new power setting.

Approach control tells us to contact the tower, and they in turn clear us to land. I call for landing flaps at five miles to touchdown. We're now in our final landing configuration and the flight engineer completes the landing checklist. At 500 feet, I call for the rudder trim to be zeroed as per NCA procedure and hold pressure on the rudder instead. The radio altimeter begins to chant '200,

100, 50, 30, 20, 10' as we near the ground. At 30 feet I begin to flare the jet and simultaneously pull back the thrust levers while releasing rudder pressure to avoid yawing as the power comes off.

A brief float and squeak, squeak, the left main gear touches the tarmac, followed closely by the right. Ground spoilers instantly rise on both wings, holding the jet firmly on the ground. We're still moving at 150 knots as I reach forward and carefully lift number 1, 3 and 4 reverse-thrust levers. After a moment's hesitation to allow the reverse vanes to move into position, I lift them to the vertical position and we're gently pushed against our shoulder straps as the engines spool up and reverse thrust rapidly slows our 747 down. At 80 knots, I stow the three reversers and start looking for a convenient high-speed taxiway to leave the runway. I exit the runway, still slowing to our taxi speed of 15 knots. As soon as the flight engineer has the auxiliary power unit running, I order him to cut engine number 2.

The moment we touched down on 34L, ATC announced 'Narita airport is closed'. Every approaching flight had already been directed to a hold and no other aircraft were moving on the ground. A team of ground vehicles instantly began inspecting 34L for signs of damage or anything that might have dropped from our wounded machine. Fifteen minutes later, Narita would be open for business again.

There are a lot of people waiting for us at our parking bay – mechanics, suits, ground handlers and the dreaded JCAB. Clearly impressed by all the brass, the marshaller gives us an extra deep bow after we shut down. Mechanics begin to gather around engine number 2 and we join them after packing up the cockpit and filling in the logbooks.

The engine looks perfectly normal and I feel a twinge of concern. Could we have screwed up somehow? Maybe there's nothing wrong with it? Less than an hour later, a borescope investigation shows some badly worn blades in the compressor section, probably

Dressed for an office visit in my 'Hans' jacket

caused by ingesting some of the gravel or rock salt that is routinely spread on Anchorage's icy runways. We're off the hook and heroes for a day but, as per the new normal in NCA, not eligible for a cash reward or even dinner. It doesn't matter; I've already promised Ed that I'm buying tonight.

Unfortunately, I wasn't off the hook with my deteriorating sinus.

Each flight seemed to make it a little worse and the ear, nose and throat physician had made it clear another elective surgery was a bad idea. Was it worth the risk of transfusion-borne diseases for a few more years of flying? Especially as I might need more blood in the future for non-elective surgery.

I don't want to sound crotchety, but each year the job had seemed less fun as bean-counters and lawyers became dominant in the struggling aviation industry. Stuff we used to do routinely was now considered a firing offence or even a crime.

NCA's grand expansion plans had already been scaled back by the twin blows of high fuel prices and declining international trade during the global financial crisis of 2007–2008. It confirmed my belief that dedicated airfreight is a cheap-fuel business. When fuel costs are high, 95 per cent of freight can be carried by container ships at a fraction of the price, and much of the remaining five per cent can be carried in the belly of passenger planes, leaving little need for special cargo flights.

In the next few months, I realised it wasn't really a choice at all. I was only 52 but I'd been aviating continuously for 34 years and my body was telling me it had simply had enough of flying. It was time to move on and experience something novel – like waking up in my own bed every morning.

My father-in-law, a wonderful self-made builder and business-man, had pulled me aside before I married his daughter and asked, 'Rob, when are you going to give up this flying nonsense and get a real job?'

Right now, father-in-law, right now.

Epilogue
by Arlene Getz

Rob never did get a 'real' job in the 30-plus years we were married. After retiring from Nippon Cargo Airlines, he went on to nurture his inventive and entrepreneurial streak. An exceptionally talented woodworker, he continued to make magnificent furniture and restore old houses. He designed items like the Grand Stand, a patented type of plate-holder that could hold items ranging in size from saucers to heavy, outsized pottery bowls. It was used in places ranging from London's Victoria & Albert Museum to up-market jewellery and craft stores in South Africa and the United States. He also wrote a series of children's books for Morgan. The first, called *Where Does Daddy Go?*, introduced Little Fly, the character who flew with Rob to show Morgan what his father did when he was away from him.

In 'retirement' Rob developed and taught classes for those afraid of flying. His course was a combination of behaviour modification and his technical expertise mixed with data about the safety of modern aviation. Many who attended his flying courses told him he'd given them the courage to get in a plane. One formerly fearful flyer later told me that whenever he got anxious before a flight, he just imagined that it was Rob in the cockpit. (He might feel differently if he reads the near-miss section of this book ...)

Always an avid cook, Rob started the Grateful Bread Baking Company with recipes that he'd created because he always said there was no decent bread in America. The bread quickly developed a loyal following in the New York food markets and stores that sold it.

Epilogue

Rob also usurped my role as the writer in the family. I'm a journalist and was working for *Newsweek* in New York when hijackers crashed planes into the World Trade Center and the Pentagon on 11 September 2001. Long before investigators dug into the background of the attackers, Rob realised that they must have trained in aircraft simulators. He promptly wrote a piece for *Newsweek*'s website on what those simulator sessions would have taught them about how to take deadly aim at the Twin Towers. In 2010 he appeared on CNN to talk about why thousands of flights had to be grounded after the eruption of Iceland's Eyjafjallajökull volcano spewed ash across international air routes. And he wrote numerous online articles bemoaning the fact that new cockpit technology meant that younger pilots no longer knew how to fly manually.

In May 2016, Rob developed a cough he couldn't shake. The doctors he saw diagnosed him first with bronchitis, then pneumonia, then pleurisy. In July, we got the hideous news that his illness was in fact mesothelioma – a rare cancer of the lung lining typically caused by exposure to asbestos. He died nine excruciating months later, on 8 April 2017.

Rob wrote this memoir before he got sick. It was, as he said in his introduction, his way of passing on his flying stories to Morgan. The idea of turning it into a book came when he discovered how much friends and family were enjoying the snippets he shared with them.

I was there for most of Rob's aviation journey. We met when we were both in a school play (I was a monkey; he was a policeman), nurtured childhood crushes on each other, drifted apart when he went to high school ahead of me and then reconnected when I bumped into him in a restaurant shortly after he joined SAA. He always used to tell me that it was a good thing I hadn't encountered him during his air force years because I probably would have refused to have anything to do with him. Based on some of these stories, he's probably right.

The voice in this memoir is quintessential Rob: a kind, modest, talented and charismatic man with a tremendous sense of humour. My contribution was to use my professional experience to do the usual editor's thing – something Rob always hated. I've done some restructuring, tightened some sentences, added in a few contextual details and checked facts and dates wherever possible.

I can't mention fact-checking without paying tribute to Rob's cousin Anthony Schapiro, whose immeasurable contribution was integral to the completion of this book. Readers will recall that Tony's career in aviation followed a near-identical trajectory to Rob's – from the SAAF to SAA to captain on an international airline (in Tony's case, Emirates). Tony's reward for that expertise was having to field my bombardments of round-the-clock WhatsApp messages asking about all matters SAAF, SAA and how to explain flying jargon to non-flying readers. It's to his enormous credit that he never flinched, not only patiently explaining the technicalities of aviation but always going a step beyond my original request. When I'd ask him if he could confirm whether Rob's quoting accurately from a checklist was word-perfect, Tony didn't just confirm – he'd track down the actual checklist and text me pictures of it. And when I'd inquire about some detail of air force procedure or life on the border, he'd contact his former air force colleagues to get as much additional information as possible. Without Tony, I'd never have known that the Recces really did keep a lion at Fort Doppies!

I'm honoured and deeply grateful that the publication of this book allows me to keep my promise to Rob that I'd share his memories.

It's been a particular pleasure to work with Jonathan Ball Publishers' editor Annie Olivier, who endeared herself to me the moment she told me Rob's stories brought her 'joy' – and who went on to show her impressive professionalism and talent in the editing of the manuscript. Thanks too to Alfred LeMaitre for his

Epilogue

meticulous copy-editing, impressive attention to detail and ability to keep tenses and measurements straight.

I also want to express my gratitude to the friends and family – too many to name here, but they know who they are – who helped us during Rob's illness and the grief that followed. Please know that no words would be adequate to express how much your support meant to me and Morgan.

Rob was a wonderful father, husband, son, brother, nephew and friend. His loss has left a wound that will never heal.

About the author

ROBERT SCHAPIRO was a professional pilot for more than 30 years. Born in Cape Town, he started his aviation career in the South African Air Force at 17. He became one of his squadron's youngest-ever commanders at 20, flying Dakotas in the Border War during the late 1970s.

In 1979 he joined South African Airways, flying Boeing 727s, 737s and 747 jumbo jets. He transferred to Japan's Nippon Cargo Airlines in 1994, flying out of New York until his retirement from aviation in 2010 as a Boeing 747 captain.

Schapiro went on to develop and teach courses to help those afraid of flying. He died of mesothelioma in 2017 at the age of 59.

Lightning Source UK Ltd.
Milton Keynes UK
UKHW020741161222
414034UK00019B/1558